Horace Carter Hovey

Guide Book to the Mammoth Cave of Kentucky

Historical, Scientific and Descriptive

Horace Carter Hovey

Guide Book to the Mammoth Cave of Kentucky
Historical, Scientific and Descriptive

ISBN/EAN: 9783337417246

Printed in Europe, USA, Canada, Australia, Japan

Cover: Foto ©Lupo / pixelio.de

More available books at **www.hansebooks.com**

TO THE

MAMMOTH CAVE

OF KENTUCKY

HISTORICAL, SCIENTIFIC, AND DESCRIPTIVE

BY

HORACE C. HOVEY

CINCINNATI

THE ROBERT CLARKE COMPANY.

1895.

MAMMOTH CAVE.

CHAPTER I.

THE pioneers who followed in the wake of Daniel
Boone, a century ago, were thrown on their own resources
in all respects. Gunpowder was one of the necessa-
ries of life for men in daily peril from wild beasts and
more savage Indians; but its importation was attended
with expense and difficulty. Hence they sent out such
strolling chemists as happened to be among them, to hunt
for niter beds. These were found in considerable quantities under the shelter of ledges at the heads of ravines.
The jutting crags reminded them of "Gothic cathedrals
and the ruins of baronial castles" (as one of them expressed himself in writing to his friends), and therefore
they called the smaller ones "Rock Houses," and the
larger ones "Rock Castles." The soil and sand-banks,
thus protected from the rains, proved to be richly impreg-
nated with the coveted saltpeter, and solid masses were
sometimes found weighing from 100 to 1,600 pounds.
Usually, however, three men would not obtain more than
from 50 to 100 pounds a day at the works.

The tools and methods used were of the most primitive
kind, and the workmen were readily induced to forsake
a niter-bed as soon as its yield grew scanty, and were con-
tinually searching for masses of pure niter, and hoping to
find veins of precious ores. This led to the exploration
of calcareous caverns, of which as many as twenty-eight
are said to have been found in Kentucky before the year
1800. A Mr. Fowler obtained from them more than

100,000 pounds of niter, and they were so far from being exhausted that, according to the estimate of local chemists, the deposits remaining in six of them exceeded 2,000,-000 pounds.

In the year 1799 a pioneer, named Baker, entered an arched opening near Crooked creek, in Madison county, about 60 miles south-east of Lexington, and proceeding a short distance under-ground, saw so many things to excite his wonder, that he returned to his cabin and took along with him his wife and three children to enjoy the further exploration. They carried with them a torch and a supply of pine splinters, but no food. Advancing about 500 yards, Mr. Baker unfortunately dropped his torch and it was extinguished. "For two days and nights this miserable family wandered in total darkness, without provision and without water, though sometimes within hearing of a cataract which they durst not approach. At length Mrs. Baker, in attempting to support herself on a rock, perceived that it was wet, and conjectured that this was caused by the mud which they had brought in on their feet. Baker immediately ascended the rock, and saw the light of day!"

This locality became known throughout the region as "the Great Cave," and was particularly described by Samuel Brown, M. D., of Lexington, in a paper read by him before the American Philosophical Society, in 1806—probably the very first of all communications of its kind in this country.

Dr. Brown describes the Great Cave as having two mouths, 646 yards apart, with a commodious passage for wagons from one to the other, the floor having the appearance of a public road that had been much frequented. The level is 80 feet above that of Crooked creek, from which its entrance is 150 yards distant. The arch varies from 10 feet to 60; and the breadth averages 40 feet, though in some parts it is 70 or 80 feet. The narrator enlarges on the scenes romantic and sublime that astonish the beholder, when the vast chambers are "sufficiently illuminated by the torches and lamps of the workmen."

The statement is made that the temperature of the cave never falls much below 52 degrees Fah., even in the coldest winter weather, and does not rise above 57 degrees at any time. To this, however, a curious exception is made, which I give in Dr. Brown's own words: " In one chamber the heat was frequently so great as to be disagreeable. The room is nearly circular and about 20 feet in diameter. The air which fills the main avenue in summer and autumn is forced into this chamber, whenever the external atmospheric air becomes so much condensed by cold as to rush into the mouth of the cave; and whenever during the winter any portion of air in the main avenue is heated by fires or lamps, as this heated air can not escape by the mouth of the cave (for the arch descends toward the mouth) it ascends into this chamber and rises to the ceiling, where it must remain." He then compares this peculiar cell to the Russian vapor bath to which Count Rumford had recently called the public attention.

Workmen dug down fifteen feet into the soil on the floor of this cave, and found it still rich in niter, although no animal remains are mentioned, nor Indian relics.

The learned authority quoted next enters into the details of preparing saltpeter for the market, claiming for it superiority to that found in Spain and India, and closes his really remarkable and historic paper with an appeal to the patriotism of Americans to make themselves independent of foreign sources of supply. " A concern for the glory and defense of our country," observes Dr. Brown, " should prompt such of our chemists as have talents and leisure to investigate this interesting subject. I suspect that we have much to learn with regard to this salt, so valuable in time of peace, so indispensable in time of war."

Had Mammoth Cave, with its immense deposits of nitrous earth, been known at the time the exhaustive description from which I have made extracts was prepared (viz., in 1806), the important fact would certainly have been recorded. I am led, therefore, to set aside the statement made by Bayard Taylor and others—I know not on what authority—that this cavern was first entered in 1802, and to accept the commonly received tradition that it was discovered by a hunter named Hutchins, in 1809, while pursuing a wounded bear. The aperture by which Hutchins entered was small at the time, and has since been considerably enlarged. It is not regarded as the original mouth, which is supposed to have been in reality the mouth of Dixon's Cave, about a quarter of a mile north of it, a magnificent hall, 120 feet high, 60 feet wide, and 1,500 feet long, as measured by me.

The first purchaser of what is now held as very valuable property, was " a small, dark, wiry man of great energy and industry," whose name was McLean, and who, for $40, bought the cave and 200 acres besides! He soon sold it to Mr. Gatewood, a brother-in-law of the founder of Bell's Tavern—that celebrated hostelry of by-gone days. After enlarging the works, Gatewood sold them to Messrs. Gratz, of Philadelphia, and Wilkins, of Lexington, Ky., who brought experience and capital to aid in developing the hidden resources of Mammoth Cave. Their agent, Mr. Archibald Miller, employed a large number of negro miners, who were reported as finding there a quantity of nitrous earth " sufficient to supply the whole population of the globe with saltpeter! "

During the war of 1812, our government being excluded from foreign sources of supply, had use for all that the miners were able to furnish under the circumstances. There were lofty mountains and interminable forests between them and the sea-board, but under the two-fold impetus of patriotism and high prices, Gratz and Wilkins, and others who embarked in the speculation, though with less brilliant success, transported thousands of pounds of the precious salt by ox-carts, and on pack-mules, mainly to Philadelphia. Let it be remembered by a grateful people that this Kentucky *salt* went far toward saving the nation in its hour of deadly peril!

The method of manufacture, as nearly as I have been able to ascertain it, was as follows: The nitrous earth was collected from various parts of the cave, by means of ox-carts for which roads were constructed that are in them-

selves surprising monuments of industry, and the soil
thus gathered was carried to hoppers of simple construction, each having a capacity of from 50 to 100 bushels.
Cold water, conveyed by wooden pipes into the cave, was
poured on the charge in each hopper, and in a day or
two a solution of the salts would run into the vats below,
whence it was pumped into a second set of pipes, tilted
so as to let the liquor flow out of the cave. After boiling
a while in the open air, it was run through hoppers containing wood ashes, the result being, if skill had been
used in mixing materials, a clear solution of the nitrate
of potash, which, having been boiled down sufficiently,
was put in troughs for cooling. In about 24 hours the
crystals were taken out ready for transportation.

Ordinary "peter dirt," as the miners called it, was expected to yield from three to five pounds of the nitrate of
lime to the bushel; and to make 100 pounds of saltpeter
it would be necessary to use 18 bushels of oak ashes, or
10 of elm, or two of ashes made by burning the dry wood
in hollow trees. It is stated that "the contract for the
supply of the fixed alkali alone, for this cave, for the year
1814, was twenty thousand dollars;" from which we may
infer the extent to which saltpeter was manufactured at
that time.

When the war was happily ended by the treaty of
Ghent, the demand for saltpeter fell off to such a degree
that Messrs. Gratz and Wilkins stopped the manufacture
at Mammoth Cave, and since then it has been valued
mainly as a place of exhibition. The original territory of
200 acres has grown to nearly 2000 acres, a portion of
which has some value for farming purposes, while other
parts are covered by heavy timber. Most of it was ac-
quired for the sake of controlling all possible entrances to
the under-lying cavern.

Mr. Archibald Miller, aided by his brothers William
and James, was the agent of Messrs. Gratz and Wilkins,
and remained at the cave to look after their interests and
to show the place to visitors. His brother-in-law, Mr.
James Moore, at one time a wealthy merchant in Phila-

delphia, took possession of the property in 1816. He became mixed up, in some manner, with the conspiracy of Burr and Blennerhassett, and was financially ruined. Gatewood again took charge of the cave for a number of years, a period not marked by any important events, either of manufacture or discovery.

Mr. Frank Gorin bought the property in 1837, employing Messrs. Moore and Archibald Miller, Jr., as his agents. The circumstance of Mr. C. F. Harvey's being lost in the cave for 39 hours, determined the proprietor to make more thorough explorations, in the course of which he found the great chamber called, in honor of him, "Gorin's Dome." He also placed Stephen and Matt, as guides, who aided in making further discoveries; so that, within the next five years, the known regions of the cave were at least trebled.

At the close of the Revolutionary war, special land grants having been made to officers and soldiers in the vicinity of Green river, Major William Croghan, a Scotchman who had distinguished himself in the United States army, was sent to survey and distribute them. His office was located at Louisville, where he also married a sister of General G. R. Clarke. He left five sons and two daughters. John, the second son, was graduated from the University of Pennsylvania, in 1813, and studied medicine with Dr. Rush, of Philadelphia, afterward taking a supplementary course at Edinburgh. During his travels in the Old World, Dr. Croghan was repeatedly asked for particulars as to the chief curiosity of his native state, and the result of his mortification at his inability to reply was that, on returning, he visited and finally purchased the Mammoth Cave. He continued the management as he found it, but expended large sums on roads, bridges and buildings. Dr. Croghan never married; and when he died, in 1845, he left the estate to trustees, to be managed for his eleven nephews and nieces, the children of Col. George Croghan, Mr. Wm. Croghan, and Gen. Thomas S. Jessup. Seven of these now survive; of whom four reside in Washington, D. C., two in New York, and one in

San Francisco. The business at the cave has been carried on by agents, among whom may be mentioned Mr. L. R. Proctor, Captain W. S. Miller, and Mr. Francis Klett, and Mr. H. C. Ganter, whose extensive improvements have made the cave more accessible, and whose urbanity and excellent regime have won many friends.

A brief description of the guides is here in place ; for while others explore these subterranean realms occasionally, these men do so daily, until they become almost identified with the rocks, rivers, and crystals found there.

Stephen Bishop, the Guide—Mammoth Cave.

The original guide, whose daring exploits and striking traits made him famous, was Stephen Bishop. He was a slave, half negro and half Indian, although the latter point is in doubt. His likeness shows him to have had intelligence and wit, and the statements of his employers and visitors agree in according to him an excellent knowledge of geology and other sciences, so far as they related to caverns. He had also a smattering of Latin and Greek, and a fund of miscellaneous information. The remains of this sable son of genius now rest beneath a cedar tree in the tangled grave-yard near the garden.

Matt and Nick Bransford, formerly slaves, were for

many years employed as guides ; but now the one is dead, and the other is retired from service on account of his infirmities. William Garvin has been a guide for twenty-six years and is a general favorite. Henry, the son of old Matt, Eddie Bishop, a nephew of Stephen, and several special guides for occasional service, are all thoroughly familiar with the ramifications of the great cavern, and ready to enliven the trip by drawing on their repertoire of jokes, original and selected. Civil and respectful as these men uniformly are, the tourist will do well to heed alike their instructions and their authority. Their prompt alacrity has saved more than one valuable life when suddenly endangered ; and it is also their duty to protect the cave property from the wanton or thoughtless injury that might otherwise be wrought by reckless hands. By special acts of the state legislature it is made a misdemeanor punishable by a fine of fifty dollars, to deface or mutilate any part of any of the several caverns on the Mammoth Cave estate, or to chip off or carry away any specimens from them. Protection is likewise extended to the trees, shrubbery, fish and game on said estate, and the manager and guides have power to see that these wise enactments are enforced. Canes, torches, fireworks, geological hammers and surveyor's instruments are for obvious reasons interdicted. Lamps are admissible, and the guides burn chemical fires at various points of interest. Choice specimens can be bought at fair prices from the hotel cabinet as souvenirs.

The early literature of Mammoth Cave is scattered through many magazines and newspapers. The oldest account that has fallen under my observation is contained in a letter from Louisville, dated July 5, 1814, and published in the *Medical Repository*, vol. xvii, pp. 391–393. It is accompanied by a map and a list of localities. The name given is the "Green River, or Mammoth Cave." The letter-writer describes a mummy " supposed to have been a queen," found a quarter of a mile from the mouth of the cave, but " lately deposited there from a neighboring cave." It is curious to note the old names. Audubon

Avenue was called "The Right-hand Chamber;" the Corkscrew, "The Mountain Room;" The Gothic Gallery, the "Sand Room;" the Gothic Avenue "The Haunted Room;" and the Chief City, "The Devil's Chamber, supposed to be ten miles from the mouth!" In the *Medical Repository*, vol. xviii, is a le'ter from Mr. Gratz, one of the owners of the great cave, and also an engraving of the famous mummy from a drawing by Rafinesque. Mr. Wilkins, the other owner, wrote an account that is to be found in the Transactions of the American Antiquarian Society, vol. I., where are also letters by S. L. Mitchill, M.D., concerning the mummies found in Kentucky and Tennessee. The oft-quoted letter of Nahum Ward, M.D., dated Marietta, O., April 4, 1816, was first published in the *Worcester Spy*, and reprinted in the *Monthly Magazine or British Register*, July, 1816, with a map of the cave and an engraving of the mummy. The "Great Kentucky Cavern" is numbered among "The Hundred Wonders of the World," in a book with that title, by Rev. E. C. Clark, published in New Haven, Conn., 1821.

A survey of the Mammoth Cave was made, in 1834–5, by Edmund F. Lee, C.E., who devoted three months to the task, and his "Map with Notes" was published by James & Gazley, of Cincinnati, O. Next came a brilliant account, in the *American Monthly Magazine*, May and June, 1837, by Robert M. Bird, M.D. (author of "Calavar"), with an engraving, by Sartain, of the mouth surrounded by the ruins of the saltpeter works. Dr. Dekay gave the first description of the blind fish (*Amblyopsis spelæus*), in 1842, see Zoology of New York, pt. 3d, p. 187. Professors Locke, Wyman, Agassiz, Silliman, and others, have at different times written communications as to the phenomena of Mammoth Cave, that have appeared in the *American Journal of Science and Art*; and an extended description of the cave fauna, by Dr. Telkampf, appeared, in 1844, with figures, in *Müller's Archiv*.

"Rambles in the Mammoth Cave, during the year 1844, by a Visitor" (supposed to be by Alexander Bullett, Esq.), with six cuts, and a map, by Stephen, the guide, was published by Morton & Griswold, of Louisville, in 1845. Collin's "History of Kentucky" (1847), contains quite a full account of this cave. "A Pictorial Guide to the Mammoth Cave," with nine cuts and eleven poems, came from the pen of Rev. Horace Martin, in 1851; and, in the same year, "An Officer of the Royal Artillery," gave a most entertaining account in *Frazer's Magazine*, republished in *Littell's Living Age*, No. 348. One still more graphic was written in 1855, by Bayard Taylor, for the *New York Tribune*, afterwards published in his "At Home and Abroad." Professor Wright's "Guide Manual" was printed in 1860, at Louisville. "The Mammoth Cave and its Denizens," by A. D. Binkerd, M.D., was published, in 1869, by Robert Clarke & Co., of Cincinnati, O. Photographs taken by magnesium and other methods, by Messrs. Waldack, Thumm, Sesser, Hains and Darnall, are on sale at the hotel as cabinet and stereoscopic views, and in fine albums. Forwood's "Historical and Descriptive Narrative of the Mammoth Cave," with twelve illustrations and a map, passed through four editions between 1870 and 1875. It is from observations made in 1867, supplemented by information derived from Messrs. Proctor and Gorin, and others, and embodies the results of much investigation. The illustrated description, by A. R. Waud, in Appleton's "Picturesque America," vol. II., pp. 540–544, is very fine, artistically considered.

The State Geological Survey of Kentucky—both the former one under Prof. D. D. Owen, and that now in progress under Prof. N. S. Shaler, with an able staff of assistants—contains valuable materials as to the cavern region of the Ohio valley. Admirable monographs on cave animals have been published by Professors Putnam, Packard, Cope, S. I. Smith and H. G. Hubbard. The latter gives a table of the fauna of Mammoth Cave, including all species described down to March, 1880. Omitting scientific details, it may be stated, in a general way, that there have thus far been described, as species peculiar to this cavern: Vertebrata, 4; Insecta, 14; Arachnida, 8; Myriapoda, 2; Crustacea, 5; Vermes, 3; Polygastric Infusoria, 8; and Phytolitharia, 5.*

* See Appendix for an account of Fauna and Flora.

To all the foregoing authorities I desire to express my obligation for facts and suggestions that have been of use in the study of the subjects treated in this volume, and in my former articles in *Scribner's Magazine* (April and Oct., 1880), and in other periodicals.

The maps made of Mammoth Cave are in themselves an interesting study. A critic would hardly recognize them as representations of the same locality. Few can appreciate the difficulties of an underground survey, amid rugged and tortuous paths, deep pits and lofty domes, all wrapped in darkness but imperfectly scattered by lamplight. Imagine a map of Pike's Peak plotted from observations taken by torchlight on a series of moonless midnights! Then, again, the singular atmospheric conditions throw doubt on the barometrical tests, though applied by men of experience. A few facts only, of this nature, seem to be agreed on, and those are mentioned in their place in another chapter. I am informed that a set of levels was run by the State Geological Survey, from Green river to Echo river, but the results, I believe, have not appeared.

It should be understood, therefore, that accuracy is not claimed for the accompanying map. The portion this side Echo river corresponds with the recent survey made by Mr. Francis Klett, conducted independently of all previous ones, and with the advantage of a long experience in the United States Geographical Survey. Yet he only claims for it an approximation to correctness, and that not in detail but in the general courses. The part beyond the rivers is modified from older surveys, with the assistance of my artist, Mr. J. Barton Smith, and may serve as an aid to the memory, if nothing more. It is not attempted to include all the 223 avenues that are said to have been explored,* and many of which are never entered by visitors.

---

* "The known avenues of Mammoth Cave amount to 223, and the united length of the whole equals 150 miles. The average width is 7 yards, and the height the same. About 12,000,000 cubic yards of cavernous space have here been excavated by calcareous waters and atmospheric vicissitudes." Owen's *Geological Survey of Kentucky*, Vol. I., page 81.

CHAPTER II.

THE cavernous limestone of Kentucky covers an area of 8,000 square miles, and varies in thickness from 10 feet to 300 or 400, the average, perhaps, being about 175 feet. This rock shows few traces of dynamic disturbance, but has been carved by acidulated water, since the Miocene epoch, into numberless caverns.

The absence of running streams is one of the striking features of the region, explained by the fact that nearly all the rivulets have long ago eaten their way through to the drainage level, and re-appear as large springs feeding rivers of considerable size. It is said that one may, in certain directions, travel fifty miles without crossing running water. The voyager along such rivers as exist, will observe, at intervals, arches in the bluffs, whence the waters of subterranean streams emerge; and should he explore these openings, he would find them the entrances to caverns ascending by tiers toward the general surface of the country. And were he to make his way from stage to stage—a thing not often possible—he would at length come out into a valley shaped like an inverted cone, along whose sides grow bushes and trees, usually matted into a dense thicket. These valleys are called " sink-holes," and they serve to drain the surface around them. These sink-holes are said to average 100 to the square mile; and, according to Shaler, the State Geologist, " there are at least 100,000 miles of open caverns beneath the surface of the carboniferous limestone in Kentucky."

It is said that there are five hundred known caves and grottoes in Edmondson county besides Mammoth Cave, the noblest specimen of them all. Several of these have gained a measure of local celebrity, but only a few of them need be mentioned here.

Salt Cave, near to the Mammoth Cave, and belonging to the same proprietors rivals it in the magnitude of some of its avenues, for the exploration of which about twelve hours are needed. It is difficult of access, however, on account of the loose and jagged rocks that have fallen from the roof; and being a dry cave, without any spring or pool, water for the trip must be carried in canteens. Its especial attraction is for the archaeologist, as it abounds in relics of prehistoric occupancy, such as fire-places, torches, piles of faggots, cast off sandals, and numerous other things described more fully elsewhere.

Short Cave, noted for the mummies found in it, in 1813, that were afterwards transferred to Mammoth Cave ; Long Cave, rich in niter beds ; Proctor's Cave, the Diamond Cave, and others in the vicinity have their admirers. But the general feeling was well expressed by one of the natives who said to me, that " to go from any other cave to Mammoth Cave, was like going from a log-cabin to a palace."

More particular mention, however, should be made of the White Cave, about half a mile from Mammoth Cave, of which it is thought really to be an arm. The exact point of communication has not yet been found, but is supposed to be with the extremity of either the Little Bat Room, or of Audubon Avenue. It is well worth visiting both on account of the beauty and variety of its stalactites, and for its interesting paleontological contents. Passing through an iron gate, we first enter an oval chamber, irregular in contour, with a low roof and a muddy floor. In a second room we find a fine piece of stalactitic drapery called the " Frozen Cascade ; " the roof is decked with pendents of all sizes ; and the floor is cut by very crooked channels, the rills in which are so transparent as to be almost invisible. Humboldt's Pillar is a stately shaft of alabaster. In a third and larger room huge masses of limestone have fallen, around which nature has kindly drawn curtains of alabaster, rudely broken through here and there by explorers trying to force their way to regions beyond. Bishop's Dome is the farthest point yet reached, a deep pit with ornate walls, into whose depths Eddie Bishop, for whom it is named, alone has thus far descended.

Some seventy years ago, a certain Mr. Clifford, a Kentuckian, exhumed from the floor of the White Cave a number of huge fossil bones, that, after passing through various hands, finally came into the possession of the Academy of Natural Sciences at Philadelphia. These curious bones, as described by Dr. Richard Harlan, were relics of the megalonyx, the bear, bison, and stag. With them, but of a presumably later time, were found a few human bones. These remains seemed to belong to the same era as those found in the Big Bone lick. "Strictly speaking," observes Dr. Harlan, "these bones were not fossilized ; they retain a very considerable quantity of animal matter, but are more brittle and are lighter than recent bones ; most of the articulating surfaces are still more or less covered with cartilage. The bones are mostly of a yellow ocherous color, and it is stated they were found on the surface of the floor of the cave." The entrance to the White Cave dips below the horizon, and was originally so small as to admit of the ingress of but one person at a time. My theory is that the animals whose bones were here found must have fallen through a sink-hole near by.

The location of Mammoth Cave is exactly 37° 14′ N. latitude, and 86° 12′ W. longitude. It is easily reached by trains on the Louisville and Nashville Railroad, passengers being transferred at the Glasgow Junction to the Mammoth Cave Railroad running to the margin of the park in front of the hotel ; a decided improvement on the old line of coaches that used to wind in and out among the sink-holes.

The hotel register shows an aggregate of from 4,000 to 6,000 visiters a year. Many of these come from the North, and a few from various parts of Europe, drawn by their curiosity to behold this far-famed locality. The majority, however, are from Louisville, Nashville, Memphis, New Orleans, and other cities of the Sunny South ; and he who wishes to meet the best types of southern society, will be sure of finding them here.

The spot is a charming resort, aside from its peculiar attraction—the cave. The region around it is a hunter's paradise, in which quail and grouse abound, and not a few wild turkeys and deer. The grounds have been laid out with taste, ornamental shrubbery being interspersed among ancient oaks, over-shadowing a well-kept lawn. Extensive gardens supply the hotel with fresh vegetables of every kind, and the table is furnished amply with whatever the season and the market may afford.

The hotel itself is an architectural curiosity. The original cabin, built by the miners in 1812, still stands and is used as a wash-house. Next came a more stylish log-house with a wide hall between two large rooms. As visitors multiplied the cabins also multiplied, until they stood in a long row. These isolated structures were, at a later day, connected with each other and weather-boarded, the halls and rooms remaining unchanged. Then a spacious frame-house was erected in front, with offices, parlors, ball-room, and other appointments in modern style. Finally wide verandas were added, having about 600 feet of covered portico. The structure thus evolved from a log-cabin germ, is shaped like the letter L, and a more airy, delightful place can not be found in the State of Kentucky! Loitering amid the long colonnade, on the evening of our first arrival, we looked out between the tall white pillars, and the night-air floating through the noble grove of aged oaks and across the blue-grass lawn, seemed redolent of romantic associations. How many thousands of tourists, savants, and lovers have here strolled in the moonlight! At 11 P. M. the band left the ball-room for the veranda, and, according to their custom, gave the signal for retiring by playing " Home, sweet home;" and the next morning, at six, the same musicians awoke us by playing "Dixie"— that tune dear to every Southern heart!

The convenience of visitors is consulted by the establishment of two principal lines of cave exploration, designated as the Long Route and the Short Route the fees for which are, respectively, three and two dollars, including the services of a competent guide, with lamps, fire-works, and all essentials. Special terms are made for tourists wishing to make a leisurely exploration, and also for large parties. Facilities are likewise furnished, if desired, for visiting White's Cave, and other caves in the vicinity.

It should be added, to correct an erroneous impression, that while guarding their property rights, the management of the cave has always encouraged scientific investigation. No restraints were laid on the members of the American Association, when they visited it, at the close of the Cincinnati meeting, except those heartily approved of by themselves. And I take this opportunity of expressing my appreciation of the aid given me by the present and the former manager, and of the faithful assistance rendered by the guides in my explorations.

Regular hours are fixed for entering the cave, and all needed attentions are paid to the general convenience of the guest. At the lamp-cabin, as the hour approaches, the guides may be seen trimming their lamps, and preparing the outfit of the visitors whom they are to escort. The lamp used is a simple affair for burning lard-oil, and swings from four wires twisted into a handle, with a tin shield to protect the hand. Each visitor is expected to carry one of these lights, but it is not given to him till he enters the cave.

The guide's appearance is unique as he stands ready for duty. No uniform is worn, but each, white or black, dresses according to his own taste. The bunch of lamps, sometimes strung on a stick if there are many of them; the flask of oil swung by the side; the oddly-shaped basket carried on the other side, containing an assortment of chemicals for illuminating the larger rooms, together with any thing else that may be needed—makes a queer *tout ensemble.*

At the ringing of a large bell the party to go in on that trip gather in the garden, clad in any dress that suits the wearer; the ladies often donning a gymnastic dress trimmed, perhaps, with spangles and tiny bells; while easy shoes, close-fitting caps, and a comfortable temper are desirable for all.

Matt., the Guide—Mammoth Cave.

The entrance to Mammoth Cave is reached by a shady path down a wild ravine, and is about 300 yards from the hotel on the bluff. Another hotel stood, formerly, in front of the entrance, but it was burned about fifteen years ago, and the scorched trees carry the scars of the fire. A plat-

form has been leveled off and furnished with rustic seats,
where, on the hottest days of mid-summer, one may enjoy
refreshing coolness. It is 118 feet below the summit of
the bluff, and 194 feet above the level of Green river,
which flows along at the distance of about half a mile, and
furnishes excellent boating and fishing for those who are
fond of such sport. The waters of this stream are remarkable for issuing mainly from caves; for which reason they
are never frozen, even in the coldest winters, and are a
refuge for steamboats and other craft, when the Ohio is
obstructed by ice.

The air, as well as the water, of the cave is of uniform
temperature the year round. The mercury in the set of
Smithsonian thermometers kept at the hotel, may have
indicated 100° when you began your walk down into this
shady dell, but at the cave's mouth it falls to 66° at noon,
and 65° at night, with very little regard to what kind of
weather the rest of the world is having. Stand on this
bench of stone and lift your hand above your head, and
there you will find the fervid heat again. The current of
cold air may be traced for a long distance before it min-
gles with the mass of common atmosphere. Within the
cave, as we shall have occasion to observe, the temperature
is several degrees lower than at the mouth.

As I have already remarked, the ancient outlet of the
subterranean region before us was through what is now
known as Dixon's Cave. A small opening on our left as
we stand facing the present entrance, points in the direction of Dixon's Cave, but the guides say there is no opening through, although persons in one cave can make themselves heard in the other, as was proved by the miners in
1812, whose picks could be heard as stated.

Mammoth Cave has a noble vestibule! Amid tulip
trees and grape-vines, maples and butternuts, fringing
ferns and green mosses, is the gate-way to this underground palace. The fingers of a rippling rill pried the
rocks apart, perhaps ages ago, and when the roof fell in,
this chasm that we see remained. The rill still runs, and
from a frowning ledge above it leaps fifty feet to the rocks

below, where it instantly disappears as if its work were done. The arch has a span of seventy feet, and a winding flight of seventy stone steps conducts us around the lovely cascade, into a roomy ante-chamber under the massive rocks.

The prevailing coolness and uniformity of temperature led the late Dr. Croghan to excavate a deep hollow here to serve as an ice-house.

The passage-way suddenly grows very narrow, at a point about 300 feet within, and here there is an iron gate made of rude bars crossing each other. This was built by Capt. W. S. Miller, in 1874, as a safeguard against secret surveys, spoliation, and the escape of fugitives from justice. Each guide carries a key, and the gate is unlocked and locked again for every party that may enter.

The current of air that had already been quite noticeable, increases to a gale as we cross the portal, so strong indeed that our lamps are blown out. This phenomenon is due to several causes operating together. The most obvious one is the difference of temperature between the air within and that without. During most of the year in this bland climate the outside air is warmer than that of the cave, and therefore the current is outward. But when it is otherwise, the current is reversed and blows into the cave. It is not necessary to assume the existence of some lower opening as a cause for a ventilating current; yet, if there are such openings, they may help to keep the air in motion.

Prof. Silliman, who visited the cave in 1852, offered still another explanation. Regarding the mouth of the cave as the only communication between the external air and the vast labyrinth of galleries stretching away for miles in the limestone, he accounts for the purity of the air on chemical principles. Calling attention to the incredibly extensive niter beds, he says: "The nitrogen consumed in the formation of the nitrate of lime must have its proportion of free oxygen disengaged, thus enriching this subterraneous atmosphere with a larger portion of the exhilarating element." The result would be that the cave-air, being both more pure and more dense than that outside, would expand and flow outward whenever pressure was lifted by a rise of temperature above its own, which remains constant.

The word for cave, both in Latin and Greek, signifies "*a breathing-place*," as if these places were the mighty lungs of Mother Earth, through which she inhales and exhales the vital air. The classic fable of Æolus also comes to mind, in which the god of storms is represented as confining all the winds in a vast cavern, where he has his throne.*

The current of air dies down, as we advance, and only a few yards beyond the Iron Gate we have no difficulty in relighting our lamps. Here we catch the last glimpse of daylight shining in through the entrance, and all that lies beyond us is in absolute darkness. A strange sensation is usually felt by the visitor at this point, and occasionally one is found who shrinks back from the journey he has undertaken. The story is told of a Scotchman who had come to America as a tourist, led to do so by the hope of seeing the great cave, as a special object of attraction ; but, when he reached this spot, and found to his surprise that *it was dark* in the cavern, he positively refused to enter!

Most visitors, however, find a certain romantic charm on entering these regions of perpetual silence, where the pleasing alternation of day and night is unknown, as is also the change of the seasons, summer and winter being alike, and vernal and autumnal airs the same. Whatever

*There are many "blowing caverns" in existence, and in some of them the blast is marvelous and inexplicable. I find the following statement in Johnson's Physical Geography, though I do not vouch for its correctness: "From a blowing cave in the Alleghany mountains, 100 feet in diameter, the current of air is so strong as to keep the weeds prostrate to the distance of sixty feet from its mouth. But the most extraordinary example is the great cave of Ouybe, of unknown extent, in central Asia. The tempests that rush from it are sometimes so violent as to carry off everything on the road into an adjoining lake! The wind coming from the interior of the earth is said to be warm in winter, and so dangerous that caravans often stop for a whole week till the tempests have subsided!"

tremendous energies may once have hurled the loose rocks
to the floor that now lie scattered around, no convulsion
has disturbed the strata for ages, and there is no safer place
above ground than is here below. The loudest thunder-
storm may roll across the heavens, but its din does not in-
vade the profound quiet of these deep vaults.

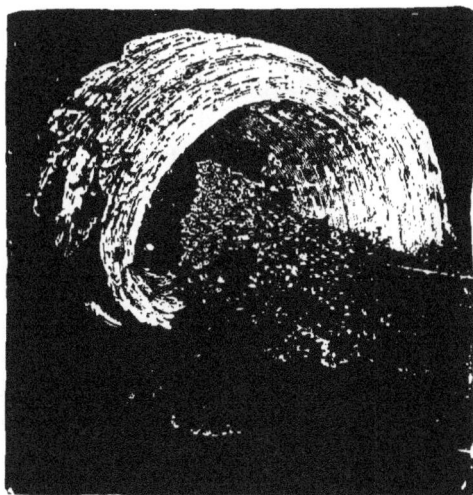

OULOPHOLITES, OR CURVED CRYSTALS OF GYPSUM.

CHAPTER III.

WHATEVER route one takes, he must traverse for a longer
or shorter distance, what is fitly designated as the MAIN
CAVE, because it is like a great trunk, from which the
avenues seem to branch. I shall, therefore, devote this
chapter to its description, together with some of the less
frequented places not now included in any regular route.

For perhaps fifty yards, after leaving the Iron Gate, the
way lies under a low ceiling, and is walled in by fragments
of rock piled up by the miners. Beyond the Narrows, as
this passage is called, and where the way grows wider,
there is a well-marked cart-road, and places where the
oxen were tied up to be fed, corn-cobs also lying scattered
around. The carts could not have been driven in through
the Narrows, but were brought in piecemeal and put together again inside. The oxen, likewise, were unyoked
and led in singly. Wooden pipes are laid in the earthen
floor, each being about 20 feet long and 10 inches in diameter, bored lengthwise and joined together by iron
bands. Such of them as were for conveying water into
the cave are decayed badly, while those used to conduct
the alkali out to the boilers are in excellent preservation.

Suddenly the roof lifts above our heads, and we are in the Rotunda, located, it is said, directly under the dining-room of the hotel. On our right are three huge vats, built of oak plank, and partly full of nitrous earth. The tall frame that once held the pump is now made useful for holding any superfluous wraps we may feel like leaving—for it is not well to be too warmly clad.

ʏ The area around us, including about half an acre, is rugged with heaps of rubbish that might have been leveled long ago, had it not been for their flavor of antiquity, and the guide's satisfaction in telling visitors that "these piles of lixiviated earth are monuments of the War of 1812!"

Looking aloft, we are impressed with a sense of the magnitude of the room we have entered, but, when we come to figures we miss the accustomed objects of comparison.

"Guess how wide this chamber is!" says the guide.

One thinks it can not be less than 150 feet : another says 200 or 250; and yet another is sure it is fully 300 feet.

"Guess how high it is!"

We look up to the dim ceiling and estimates vary again. To one it seems 50, to another 80, to a third, 100 feet high.

The lack of charity shown for errors in guesswork is sometimes very amusing to one who has used the tape-line in underground surveys, and knows how easy it is to be deceived in mere estimates of distances. The atmosphere of the cave is optically pure; *i. e.* no motes nor dust floats in it, and therefore the rays of light are not distributed as in ordinary air; while at the same time, as it is also chemically pure, the lamps burn very brightly. This combination of causes leads to a confusion of ideas as to the nearness or remoteness of objects.

Apply the tape-line to those two arches that open out from the Rotunda. One is found to have a span of 46, and the other of 70 feet! Our path lies through the latter, but let us make a brief digression into the other that trends away to the right.

This is Audubon's Avenue, so named in honor of the famous naturalist. It used to be called Big Bat Room, and the branch from it, running to Crevice Pit, was called

Little Bat Room—a title that clings to it yet. Here myriads of bats take up their winter quarters, congregating for the purpose from all the region around. Deposits of bat-guano abound, and this is supposed to be connected with the quantities of nitrous earth, which is richest here. Not a stone in these two rooms but what has been upturned for "peter-dirt;" and one can not refrain from admiring the energy and diligence of those old-time miners. Audubon's Avenue, as measured by me, is three quarters of a mile long, to where it ends in a group of stalactites. It is seldom visited.

The miners are said to have exhumed two skeletons, in 1811, in the Rotunda, at the entrance to Audubon's Avenue: one, that of a child; the other of a giant seven or eight feet in height! Mr. Gorin, as quoted by Dr. Forwood, states positively, that "no mummies were ever found in Mammoth Cave; and that no bones, either human or of the lower animals, except the two skeletons already spoken of, were ever found therein."

Before proceeding further, it may be as well to speak of the temperature of Mammoth Cave. It has been roughly estimated that twelve million cubic yards of limestone have been displaced by this immense excavation; and the importance occurred to me of ascertaining *exactly* the temperature of such a body of subterraneous air. On inquiry I learned that this had never been accurately done.

Hence I made a series of observations in 1878, that satisfied me of the need of still more careful work. Accordingly, in 1881, armed with two standard thermometers, one a Casella from the Kew Observatory, England, and the other a Green from Winchester Observatory at New Haven, Conn., I took a number of observations with the utmost care. Among my conclusions were the following: That the highest degree reached at any time in any part of Mammoth Cave is 56° Fah.; and the lowest 52½° Fah.: the mean for summer being 54°, and for winter, 53°. The latter is probably the true temperature of the earth's crust in the region where this cave is located.

The above conclusions are confirmed by the readings of an ordinary thermometer placed by Mr. Klett in the Rotunda and left there till it was, so to speak, acclimated. This gentleman reports, as the result of almost daily inspection by himself or the guides, that during the period of six months, the mercury did not rise above 54° nor fall below 53° Fah., the fair inference being, that there was not, at any time, a variation of more than one degree !*

At a point some distance beyond the Rotunda, and exactly half a mile by my pedometer, from the top of the hill, the guide calls our attention to a shelf of rock on the left, and informs us that there is the entrance to "The Corkscrew." This is a short-cut by which visitors, on returning from the Long Route, save themselves a mile or two of traveling.

Advancing in the Main Cave, we pass under over-hanging ledges called the Kentucky Cliffs, and about four feet from the floor we examine a cluster of little openings, like pigeon-boxes, that show the peculiar action of the water by which they were eaten out.

We next come to the Methodist Church, about eighty feet in diameter and forty feet high, where those ancient

*As this is a matter that has been under dispute, former observations by scientific observers having agreed on 59° Fah. as the correct temperature, I give below a table of my main observations, which were most carefully made with practically perfect instruments, on the 13th, and 15th days of August, 1881 :

At the hotel on the hill the mercury indicated	92 deg.	Fah.
At the mouth of the cave (at noon)	65½ "	"
" " " (7 P. M.)	60 "	"
At the Iron Gate, 100 yards within, where the current is strongest	52½ "	"
In the Rotunda (1.000 yards within)	53 "	"
In Audubon's Avenue	54 "	"
In Little Bat Avenue	54 "	"
In the Gothic Avenue (oldest and driest portion)	56 "	"
In Richardson's Spring (in the water)	54 "	"
In the Arched Way	54½ "	"
At the Bottomless Pit (top)	54 "	"
" " (midway)	56 "	"
" " (at the bottom)	53 "	"
In the Mammoth Dome (top, 250 feet above bottom)	54 "	"
" " (midway)	53½ "	"
" " (bottom)	53 "	"
At the Echo River (in the water)	55 "	"
" " (in the air)	56 "	"
" " (where it empties in Green River)	58 "	"

miners used to hear the Gospel preached by itinerant min-
isters, who sought their welfare. The logs that served for
benches are still in position, and many a sermon has been
delivered from the rocky pulpit since the days of the pioneer worshipers. The writer can not soon forget a re-
ligious service he had the privilege of attending in this
natural temple, one summer Sabbath. The band did duty,
as orchestra, the guests and guides were seated around the
pulpit in decorous order, the servants from the hotel were
a little in the back-ground, the walls were hung with a
hundred lamps, and the scene itself was beautiful. Then
the psalm arose, led by the instruments, and waves of har-
mony rolled through those rocky arches till they died
away in distant corridors. The text from which the cler-
gyman, himself a visitor, wove his discourse was peculiarly
adapted to the place and the occasion: John xiv: 5, "*How
can we know the way?*"

For the next 150 yards the old cart ruts run between
mountainous heaps of "lixiviated earth," and the hoof-
prints of the oxen remain as if they had lately drawn loads
to the hoppers. Here are more ruins of niter-works, eight
huge vats, lines of wooden pipes, pump-frames, and other
signs of former activity. What a busy set those old fellows must have been! One can almost credit their boast
that they could dig saltpeter enough from Mammoth Cave
to supply the whole world.

Leaving, for the present, the Gothic Galleries, where
these ruins lie, we pursue our way under the Grand Arch,
about sixty feet wide and fifty high, and extending for
many hundred feet. On our left are the Standing Rocks,
four in number, thirty feet long, and weighing may be
twenty tons apiece. What a shaking there must have
been when they fell from the lofty arch above and buried
themselves in this upright position in the earthen floor!

New objects of interest meet us at every step, as we advance. During a moment's pause we are startled by what
seems the loud ticking of a musical time-piece. It is but
the measured melody of water dripping into a basin hidden behind the rocks. It is only a small basin, and the

drops fall but a few inches, yet such are the acoustic effects of the arch that they can be heard for a long ways, as they monotonously fall, drop by drop, just as, perhaps, they have fallen for a thousand years.

Not far from this natural water-clock, is a symmetrical recess chiseled by a tiny rill, whose limpid water is collected in a pool. The story is told of a blind boy who rambled over the country, winning a precarious living by his violin, and who, as he said, was resolved *to see* the cave for himself. He lost his way, and when found by his companions, was quietly sleeping beside this basin, which ever since has been called "Wandering Willie's Spring."

Singular effects are produced by the devices of the guides. At certain spots wonderful shadow profiles are cast by the projecting buttresses. One long admired was that of George Washington. But it is now eclipsed by what is styled the bust of Martha Washington, which really is a magnificent illusion. The guests are stationed under the Grand Arch, and their lamps withdrawn. Then at a place 550 yards distant, the guide burns magnesium, he himself being out of sight, and the result is the remarkable effect described. What we behold seems to be a sculptured mass of Parian marble instead of simply a mass of white light amid the rocks.

The incrustations of gypsum stained by the black oxide of manganese, seem to cut gigantic silhouettes from the ceiling of creamy limestone. At first we ridicule these fancies, but at last they fascinate us. Wild cats, buffaloes, monkeys and ant-eaters—indeed, a whole menagerie is on exhibition, including the old mammoth himself, and Barnum's fat girl. There is an especially fine side-show of a giant and giantess playfully tossing papooses to and fro.

It is well to observe the large rock on our right very carefully, not only for the interest it excites by its singular resemblance to a mighty sarcophagus, but because the Giant's Coffin, as it is called, is one of the most important land-marks in the cave. It equals in size one of the famous blocks of Baalbek, being forty feet long, twenty wide, and eight or more deep. Often as I have passed it,

whether alone or with a hundred companions, it has ever
been with a feeling as if I had intruded into some sacred
mausoleum.   This ponderous rock hides behind it the
crevice that, until recently, was the only known way of
access to the wonderful region of pits, domes and rivers,
that we are to visit another day.

THE GIANT'S COFFIN.

At a point 100 yards beyond the Giant's Coffin, the
trend of the Main Cave turns upon itself at an acute angle,
on the left, and sweeps around in a magnificent amphitheater on the right.   This enchanting place should not be
hastily passed.   The effect of fire-works here is remark-
ably brilliant, and the sublime scene thus illumined is one
to be remembered long.

The apex of the acute angle is marked by McPherson's
monument, a rude pile of stones in memory of a gallant
soldier.   More than 300 such monuments have been erected
in different portions of the cave, in honor of various indi-
viduals, literary institutions, and the several States of the
Union.   Some of these pillars reach from floor to roof,
each tourist who chooses to do so, adding a stone.   An

incidental benefit of the custom is that it has helped to clear the paths.

A Strange Sanitarium.

The roofless remains of two stone cottages are next visited, as having a melancholy interest on account of their history. These, and ten frame ones, now torn down, were built in 1843 for the use of fifteen consumptive patients, who here took up their abode, induced to do so by the uniformity of the temperature, and the highly oxygenated air of the cave, which has the purity without the rarity of the air at high altitudes. The second stone house was a dining-room; all the rest were lodging rooms, and were well furnished. The cottages were not all at this spot. One was about 100 yards within Audubon's Avenue; in which a Mr. Mitchell, from South Carolina, lived for five months, and then died. He was buried in the little cemetery near the cave, and his body was afterward taken away. The next cottage was near Wandering Willie's Spring. Still another was erected in Pensico Avenue. All the others, nine in number, stood in a line, about 30 feet apart, extending from the acute angle onward. The experiment was an utter failure; as was also the pitiful attempt on the part of these poor invalids to make trees and shrubbery grow around their dismal huts. The open sunshine is as essential to rosy health as it is for green leaves.

The salubrity of the cave, so far as its effects on the spirits and health of visitors are concerned, is decidedly marked. The air is slightly exhilarating, and sustains one in a ramble of five or ten hours, so that at its end he is hardly sensible of fatigue. In one of the earliest accounts of the cave, published in 1832, it is said that "the niter diggers were a famously healthy set of men;" and that, on humanitarian grounds, it was customary to employ laborers who were in feeble health, "who were soon restored to good health and strength, though kept at constant labor; and more joyous, merry fellows were never seen." It certainly is noticeable that most tourists, whether it is due to the delicious air or some other happy cause, generally mingle a jocund feeling with the awe and solemnity that one would suppose should be awakened by scenes so sublime.

A strangely beautiful transformation scene is exhibited in the Star Chamber, a hall from 200 to 500 feet long (according to the place you measure from), about 70 feet wide at the floor and narrowing to 40 at the ceiling, which is 60 feet above our heads. The light gray walls are in strong contrast to the lofty ceiling coated with black gypsum; and this, again, is studded with thousands of white spots, caused by the efflorescence of the sulphate of magnesia. The guide bids us seat ourselves on a log bench by the wall, and then collecting our lamps, vanishes behind a jutting rock; whence, by adroit manipulations, he throws shadows, flitting like clouds athwart the starry vault. The effect is extremely fine, and the illusion is complete. The ceiling seems to have been lifted to an immense distance, and one can easily persuade himself that by some magic the roof is removed, and that he looks up from a deep cañon into the real heavens.

"Good night," says the guide, "I will see you again in the morning!"

With this abrupt leave-taking he plunges into a gorge, and we are in utter darkness. Even the blackest midnight in the upper world has from some quarter a few scattered rays; but here the gloom is without a gleam. In the absolute silence that ensues one can hear his heart beat. The painful suspense is at length broken by one of those outbursts of laughter that come when least expected: and then we ask each other the meaning of this sudden desertion. But, while thus questioning each other, we see in the remote distance a faint glimmer, like the first streak of dawn. The light increases in volume till it tinges the tips of the rocks, like the tops of hills far away. The horizon is bathed in rosy hues, and we are prepared to see the sun rise, when all at once the guide appears, swinging his cluster of lamps, and asking us how we like the performance. Loudly encored, he repeats the transformations again and again,—starlight, moonlight, thunderclouds, midnight and day-dawn, the latter heralded by cock-crowing, the barking of dogs, lowing of cattle, and various other farm-yard sounds; until, weary of an entertainment that long ago lost its novelty for him, he bids us resume our line of march.

It is doubtful if one visitor in fifty goes farther into the Main Cave than to the Star Chamber; but none fail to see this favorite hall of illusions. The path to it is dry and so well-trodden as to be quite dusty.

A pleasing incident comes to mind, showing how easily it may be reached, although a mile under ground. One evening, after tea, I had entered thus far alone, without a guide, and after studying for a while the peculiar effects of light and shade, I sat down on the log bench and put my lamps out, in order to enjoy the luxury of darkness, silence, and solitude. But ere long voices were heard, and mysterious peals of laughter. Soon the day-dawn effect was unexpectedly produced, by the approach of a party of jocund youths and maidens, with lights, who, having dressed for a hop, first paid a visit to this enchanted ground; and, as cave dust never flies nor sticks, they did so without a speck on polished boot or trailing robe.

It may be well to say here that the remainder of the Main Cave is one of the "Special Routes," and those who wish to visit it should make their arrangements for doing so at the start.

As we pass along under a mottled ceiling that changes, from the constellation just described, to a mackerel sky with fleecy masses of floating clouds, many curious objects are pointed out to us. Here is a stout oak pole, projecting from a crevice, now inaccessible—put there when, and by whom, and for what purpose? There are snow-drifts of native Epsom salts, whitening the dusky ledges. Spaces are shown, completely covered by broad slabs, underneath which are the ashes and embers of ancient fires. Side-cuts occasionally tempt us from the beaten path, into which we return by a circuitous way. These are generally short, though some of them are several hundred yards long.

Proctor's Arcade, the next considerable enlargement beyond the Star Chamber, is said to be 100 feet in width, 45 in height, and three-quarters of a mile in length. Its proportion are very symmetrical throughout, and when illuminated by blue lights, burning at several points, deserves the encomium pronounced on it by Dr. Wright, of being "the most magnificent natural tunnel in the world."

Kinney's Arena is a hall about 100 feet in diameter, and 50 feet in height. Here another stick in the ceiling is pointed out, concerning which there has been much speculation.

After passing the S Bend, which has no special points of interest, we enter a spacious chamber, thus described by Prof. C. A. Wright, in whose honor it is named:

"Wright's Rotunda is 400 feet in its shortest diameter. The ceiling is from 10 to 45 feet in height, and is perfectly level, the apparent difference in height being produced by the irregularity of the floor. It is astonishing that the ceiling has strength to sustain itself." "When this immense area is illuminated at the two extremes, simultane-

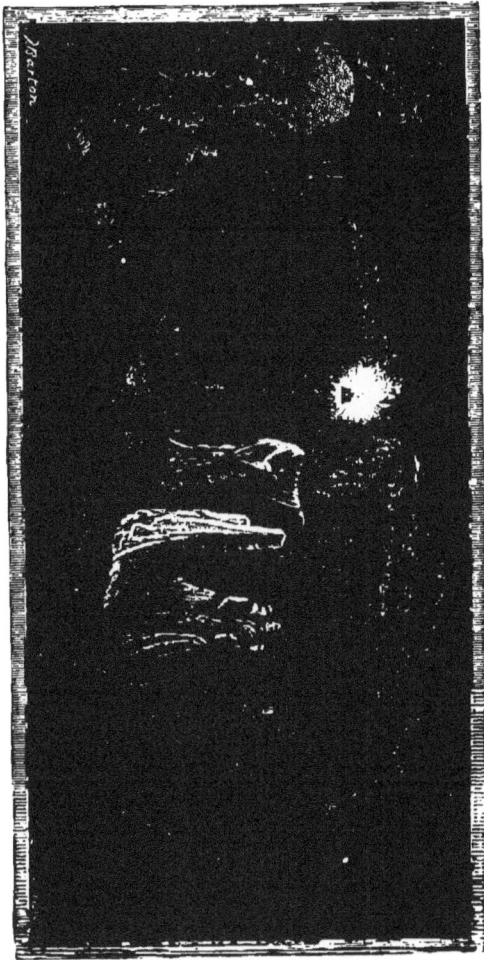

Marriage Scene in Gothic Chapel.

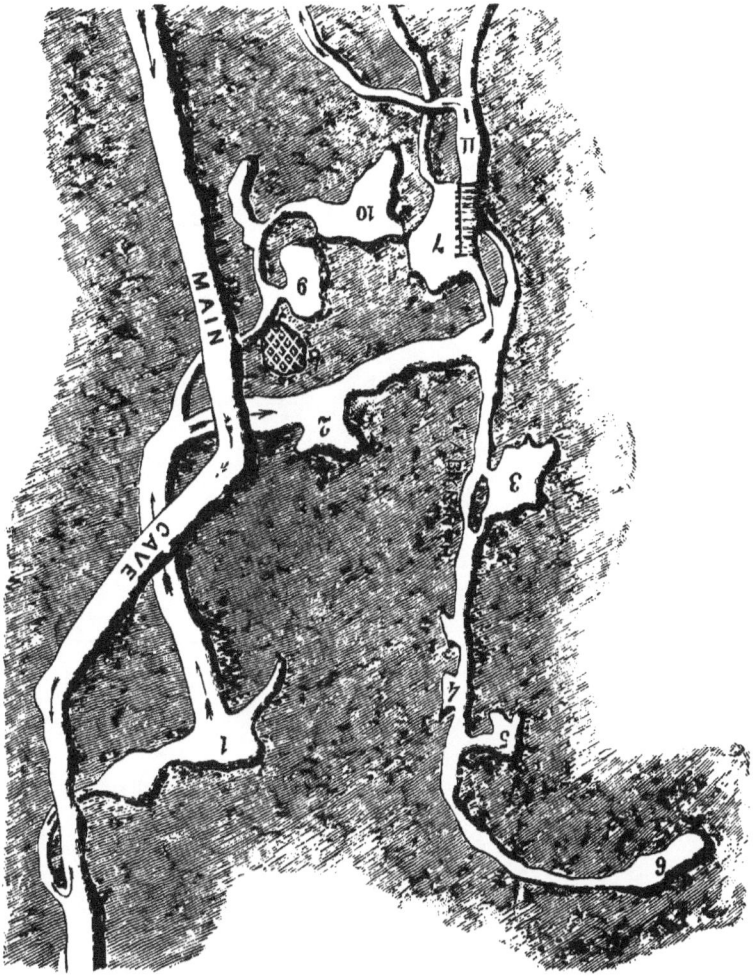

The Labyrinth in Mammoth Cave.

1. Wooden Bowl Room.
2. Side Saddle Pit.
3. Gorin's Dome.
4. Putnam's Cabinet.
5. Hovey's Cabinet.
6. Ariadne's Grotto.
7. Bottomless Pit.
8. Covered Pit.
9. Scylla.
10. Charybdis.
11. Revellers' Hall.

ously, it presents a most magnificent appearance." Nicholas' Monument, named for one of the guides, stands at one end of this large hall, a column four feet in diameter and extending from the floor to the ceiling.

In this part of the cave the path, which I have said was very free from incumbrances, grows extremely rough, and the floor is but a bed of angular blocks, over which we make slow progress. We are willing to take the guide's word for it that Fox Avenue is worth exploring, and that various other spots are curious or beautiful.

We clamber over the big rocks, however, to survey a mass of ruins known by the ominous name of the Black Chambers. The walls and ceilings are here completely coated with black gypsum. We find that the funereal darkness defies magnesium, and refuses to be cheered even by red fire.

Crossing to the right hand side from these baronial ruins, we ascend through the Big Chimneys to an upper level, and, as we proceed, we hear the sound of a waterfall, which increases as we draw near, until we find ourselves at the Cataracts.

I have never happened to see this spot except in a dry season, and then, although there is quite a cascade, there is nothing to correspond with the frightful torrents that are said to pour down after heavy rains, " with a roar that resounds afar, and seems to be shaking the cave itself from its foundations." The water, be it more or less, falls from large perforations over-head, and is instantly lost to sight in a deep, funnel-shaped pit.

No creeping nor crawling has to be done in the Main Cave, the average width, throughout its entire extent being about 60 feet, and its height about 40 feet; the length is estimated at nearly four miles, of which we have, thus far, traversed less than half.

For the sake of variety, let us digress to visit the Solitary Chambers; to reach which we have to pass for perhaps 20 feet under a low arch. Pursuing our way across these lonely apartments, we finally, by dint of much crawling, arrive at the Fairy Grotto, once famous for its ten thousand stalactites, as varied in form as the shapes visible in the kaleidoscope. Ruthless hands have marred this beautiful place, demolishing its exquisite creations, until it is difficult to realize the truth of the earlier descriptions.

Entering the Main Cave again, near the Cataracts, we continue our walk, clambering over great masses of fragments, taking care not to break our necks, until we find ourselves beyond this rocky pass, and under the stupendous vault known as the Chief City. Amid its wonders we linger long. Bayard Taylor's estimate of this colossal room shows the vigor of his imagination: "Length, 800 feet; breadth, 300 feet; heighth, 125 feet; area, between 4 and 5 acres!" Another, whose imagination was still more lively, estimates the area at 11 acres! There probably are about *two* acres; but the reader who has never explored this underground realm, will find it tax his mind to realize how large even such an area would seem, clothed with eternal night, built in by walls of massive rock, and over-arched by so vast a dome as to make us hold our breath, lest if silence were broken it would fall.

" Why doesn't it fall? " I heard a timid visitor ask the guide.

" I know of no reason why it should not fall at this very moment," said he, solemnly, " and I never come underneath without some degree of fear. Yet the arch appears to be a solid, seamless block of limestone, and it may stand for a thousand years."

Immense rocks are thrown about in the wildest confusion, and it is evident that mighty forces were once here at play. But all is quiet now, and the dust of ages lies on those huge blocks. The guide picks out from interstices between the stones, half-burnt bits of cane, which he assures us the red men used to fill with bear's fat and burn, in lieu of torches, to light them in their solemn councils, or during their search for hidden treasures of flint or alabaster. The fact that no weapons have ever been found here shows that the councils held were of a peaceful nature; and the absence of human remains proves that they were not here on a funereal errand. But certain it is that Indian chiefs saw this city centuries before we saw the light of day. It should be added, concerning the cane torches, that although now comparatively few, they were formerly so numerous as to furnish materials for hundreds of bon-fires by which the guides were accustomed to illuminate the mountain and the dome. Dr. Bird speaks (in 1837) of the supply as inexhaustible, filling the rocky crevices in " astonishing, unaccountable quantities."

The stern features of the scene are best surveyed from the summit of a rugged ascent, called quite appropriately, a mountain. Here we sit, while, again and again, the guide lights red fire and burns Roman candles, and discharges rockets that find ample room to explode before they strike the far-distant walls. The probability is that electric lamps will be placed, at an early day, in these dim regions, and then every nook and secret recess will be brought into view; but it is doubtful if the picturesque effects could be heightened beyond those now caused by the pyrotechnic glare that, as it flashes and dies away, over the long slope of irregular rocks, and athwart the gigantic vault, brings to view such glories as no torch-bearing mound-builder ever saw or dreamed of seeing.

The majestic dome appears to follow us, as we retire from it, overarching us at every step; as is the case with the sky, that bends the same canopy of blue above every meadow and valley, as the traveler moves from place to place. This phenomenon, first noticed by Mr. E. F. Lee, affords an impressive proof of its symmetrical proportions and vast dimensions.

And while the crimson light stains the arches and pinnacles, we take leave, with many a backward look, of this prehistoric council-chamber of sagamores and dusky braves.

Resolute pedestrians may cross the Chief City, and explore St. Catherine's City—which presents few novelties— and then go on under overhanging cliffs, to a place where, beneath a ceiling about fifteen feet high, the cave spreads out to a considerable width, and curious botryoidal formations grow. This branch ends in Symmes' Pit, a well thirty feet deep. The Blue Spring Branch is a long passage, with very rough going, that leads on to a place where the rocks fill the cave from floor to roof, hopelessly obstructing further progress. And this is the end of the Main Cave.

SALTPETER VATS.

CHAPTER IV.

THE Short Route may be taken either by day or by night, as suits the convenience of the visitors; but those coming for a brief stay prefer the latter, as it leaves the entire ensuing day for the longer journey. The time required is four hours; hence those who enter at 7 P. M. may expect to come out again by 11 P. M., and with no more fatigue than will insure a sound night's rest in a hotel where a mosquito never has been seen, and where locks and bolts are only ornamental.

Passing without further mention points already described in the preceding chapter, we pause first at the Gothic Gallery. Here in the foreground are the old vats and pump-frames; and a stairway beyond them leads to the gate of a long avenue we are shortly to explore. From this ample gateway a narrow gallery, or rocky shelf, sweeps entirely across the Main Cave—really forming a bridge, whereby one might pass to the other side. Should he do so, he would find indications that this was once a continuance of the avenue, and both representing the highest level known in the cave. Taken as a whole, the amphitheater is a noble one, and you are not surprised to be informed that here Edwin Booth once rendered selections from the play of Hamlet, taking yonder rocky platform on the right as his temporary stage. Fire-works are generally exhibited here, and to great advantage.

Ascending the steps we enter the Gothic Arcade, and after proceeding about forty yards, our attention is directed to a niche in the left hand wall, which we are told is the Seat of the Mummy. The legend is that here were once found the dried bodies of a woman and a child, unlike modern Indians, and probably belonging to some extinct and ancient race. Such conflicting statements have been published concerning these remains, that many have classed the " Mammoth Cave Mummy " with the numerous hoaxes with which ingenious perversity has amused itself at the expense of a credulous public. The facts are these:

In 1813 a scientific visitor, probably Mr. Merriam, of Brooklyn, N. Y., saw what he mentions as "a relic of ancient times, which requires a minute description." This description is substantially as follows: That some miners had exhumed a female body while digging saltpeter-earth in the Short Cave (not any portion of the Mammoth Cave, but a small cave in the neighborhood). The grave was covered by a flat rock, and contained the wardrobe, as well as the body of the woman. The latter was in a sitting posture, with the arms folded, and hands crossed and bound by a small cord. The inner wrapping was made of two deer-skins, closely shaved and ornamented with vines and leaves marked in white. Next came a woven sheet, in texture like fabrics made by the South Sea Islanders. The hair on the mummy's head was red and clipped within an inch of the skin. The teeth were white and perfect; the nails long; the features regular; the color dark but not black; the body free from blemish, except a wound between the ribs and an injury to one eye; the frame that of a person about 5 feet 10 inches in height; the flesh hard and dry upon the bones; and the weight, at the time of discovery, but 14 pounds, though it gained 4 pounds more by absorbing dampness. A knapsack, a reticule, and a pair of moccasins, all of woven or knit fiber, lay by the mummy's side. The articles contained in the reticule and knapsack were head-dresses of feathers; a cap of woven

bark ; several hundred strings of beads tied up in bunches ;
a necklace of red hoofs of fawns ; an eagle's claw and the
jaw of a bear; folded skins of rattlesnakes ; vegetable
colors done up in leaves ; bunches of sinews, thread, and
twine ; seven needles (or awls) ; a deer-skin hand piece, to
protect the hand in sewing ; and two whistles of cane,
bound together by a cord.   After explaining that the cause
of such perfect preservation was not due to any embalm-
ing process, but merely to the antiseptic properties of the
nitrous earth, combined with the extreme dryness of the
cave, this writer concludes his fanciful description, by say-
ing, "The features of this ancient member of the human
family much resembled those of a tall, handsome American woman.   The forehead was high, and the head well
formed."

This same mummy was found by Dr. Nahum Ward, of
Marietta, O., in 1815, in the Gothic Avenue (according to
Mr. Proctor, a former proprietor of the hotel), and sent
by him to the Antiquarian Society of Worcester, Mass.,
where it now is.   The gentleman to whom the credit of
finding is really due, was Mr. Charles Wilkins, of Lexington, Ky., one of the owners of Mammoth Cave.   In a letter dated October 2, 1817, in reply to the inquiries of the
secretary of the Antiquarian Society, Mr. Wilkins first
describes the mummy of an infant about one year old,
found in a cave about four miles from Mammoth Cave,
and which, with its clothing, had been thrown into the
furnace by the workmen.   He regretted this so much as
to offer a reward for the next that might be found.   The
result was the discovery, a month later, of the one that
was afterwards sent to Worcester.   His agent (Mr. Miller)
sent for it and placed it, for safe-keeping, in the Mammoth Cave, and quite possibly he laid it in the niche of
the Gothic Avenue that is now pointed out ; but this
is doubted by some.   Wilkins, in a matter of fact style
quite in contrast with the flowing sentences of Merriam,
tells the same story, confirming the account of the uten-
sils, ornaments, and articles of dress.

Samuel L. Mitchill, M. D., of New York, also wrote to

the Secretary, giving an account of other mummies from the caverns of Kentucky and Tennessee. His letter is dated, August 24, 1815, and is preserved in the published Transactions of the Antiquarian Society. He states that " In exploring a saltpeter cave near Glasgow, several human bodies were found enwrapped carefully in skins and cloths." He particularly describes one that had "a deep and extensive fracture of the skull, near the occiput, which probably killed him."

In the Medical Repository (vol. XVIII. p. 187), is published, a letter from Mr. Gratz, one of the owners, accompanying a parcel of curiosities sent to Dr. Mitchell, from which we may fairly conclude that, besides interlopers from Short Cave and elsewhere, there were genuine Mammoth Cave mummies. Mr. Gratz says:

" There will be found in this bundle two moccasons, in the same state they were when dug out of the Mammoth Cave, about 200 yards from its mouth. Upon examination, it will be perceived that they are fabricated out of different materials; one is supposed to be a species of flag, or lily which grows in the southern parts of Kentucky; the other of the bark of some tree, probably the pawpaw. There are also, in this packet, a part of what is supposed to be a kinniconeke pouch, two meshes of a fishing net, and a piece of what we suppose to be the raw material, and of which the fishing net, the pouch and one of the moccasons are made. All of which were dug out of the Mammoth Cave, nine or ten feet under the ground; that is, below the surface or floor of the Cavern." Mr. Gratz also describes " an Indian bowl, or cup containing about a pint, cut out of wood, found also, in the Cave;" and adds " lately there has been dug out of it the skeleton of a human body, enveloped in a matting similar to that of the pouch."

During the progress of the recent State geological survey, Prof. F. W. Putnam, through his connection with it, was able to examine the archæology of the various rock shelters and caverns of Kentucky; and his report was published in 1875, in the Proceedings of the Boston Society of

Natural History. He collated all known facts concerning
the relics here mentioned; examined the celebrated mummy in the museum at Worcester, finding ample proof of
the general correctness of the earlier accounts; and also
exhibited exceedingly curious fabrics from Salt Cave, a
small cave near Mammoth Cave, and belonging to the
same proprietors.

Indian fire-places, with ashes and embers remaining;
imprints of feet shod with braided moccasons or sandles,
as distinct as if made but a few days previous; numerous
cast-off sandles, artistically braided from the leaves of the
cat-tail flag; woven cloth, dyed with black stripes, and in
one corner showing that it had been mended by darning;
bunches of bark, and pieces of bark-twine and rope;
fringes and tassels of fibers; wood cut by a stone ax; a
few arrow-heads, and various fragments—these were
among the curiosities found by Prof. Putnam in the Salt
Cave. It is to be hoped that this enthusiastic lover of science may find his example of thorough research imitated
by those who do not have to travel a thousand miles to do
their cave hunting!

On the old maps of the cave the Gothic Avenue is put
down as the Haunted Chamber, on account of an adven-
ture that befell one of the saltpeter miners. The story runs
that a raw hand disdained the guidance of an older work-
man, and trudged off alone to dig his lot of "peter-dirt,"
and was forgotten by the other miners until dinner time.
Then a few negroes, half-naked, as was their custom when
working, started to hunt him up. The poor fellow had
filled his salt-sacks and started back, but finding the way
longer than it had seemed when going in, concluded that
he was lost. In his fright he became thoroughly bewildered, and, to make matters worse, fell over a stone and
put his lamp out. His sins came in remembrance, and he
gave himself up to alternate frenzy and prayer. "It was
at this moment," says Dr. Bird, who tells the story, "that
the miners in search of him made their appearance; they
lighted upon his sack, lying where he had thrown it, and
set up a great shout, which was the first intimation he had

of their approach. He started up, and seeing them in the distance, the half-naked negroes in advance, all swinging their torches aloft, he, not doubting they were the identical devils whose appearance he had been expecting, took to his heels, yelling lustily for mercy. Nor did he stop, notwithstanding the calls of his amazed friends, until he had fallen a second time over the rocks, where he lay on his face, roaring for pity, and only by dint of much pulling and shaking was he convinced that he was still in the world and in the Mammoth Cave!"

The Post Oak is a pillar about twelve feet high, bearing some resemblance to a trunk of a tree, and is formed by the meeting of a stalactite and stalagmite. It stands at the entrance of the Register Hall, on whose smooth ceiling hundreds of names have been inscribed in lampblack, before the rules of the cave had prohibited that cheap method of gaining immortality. As a substitute for this rocky album, convenient places are provided for visitors to leave their cards, which, in this extremely dry portion of the cave, will remain fresh and uninjured for many years. Thousands of cards, from all parts of the world have thus been left, and it affords amusement to look over them. Here are also many memorial heaps erected by admirers of celebrated persons, each pile having a sign to show in whose honor it stands, and by whom it was erected.

On reaching what are called the Pillars of Hercules, the guide collects the lamps and arranges them with fine effect among the arches of the Gothic Chapel, which he then invites us to enter. The roof of this room seems to rest on groups of stalagmitic columns, once beautiful, no doubt, but now sullied by sacrilegious smoke. I counted eight, and found fragments of thirty more of them. Their growth was slow, requiring centuries to develop their present dimensions; but I can hardly accept the conclusion of Dr. A. D. Binkerd that 940,000 years were needed for their completion. It should be remembered that the rate of increment varies with changing conditions. Some of them are still dripping slowly, while others are perfectly dry. Hence any estimate as to their age in years is idle and fruitless. It is only certain that they are *very old*.

Three pillars are so grouped as to form two Gothic arches, and before this unique altar once stood a runaway bride who had promised an anxious mother that she would "never marry any man on the face of the earth." She kept the letter of her promise, but was married after all to the man of her choice, in this novel Gretna Green. Several romantic marriages have since been celebrated here.

This entire avenue is more than a mile long, and abounds in grotesque curiosities. The Old Arm Chair is a stalagmite resembling the object for which it is named; and one of a lively fancy might say the same of the Elephant's Head. Other objects pointed out are Vulcan's Shop, the Lover's Leap, Gatewood's Dining Table, Lake Purity, and Napoleon's Dome—grand in its symmetry and size. The avenue ends in a double dome and a small cascade.

Retracing our steps to the Main Cave, and proceeding as far as the Giant's Coffin, we leave it again, by a crevice behind that huge sarcophagus, and presently find ourselves in the Deserted Chambers, in one of which was found the wooden bowl mentioned by Mr. Gratz. The opening on the left is called Ganter Avenue for Mr. H. C. Ganter, whose skill and perseverance have made the passage available. It is indeed a combination of avenues on three different cave-levels, and it winds about in the most extraordinary manner. In March, 1891, it was surveyed by Mr. Ben Hains and myself, and found to be 8,500 feet long. There are at least 200 changes of direction, but the general trend is for the first 6,000 feet to the south-east, and thence to the westward for about 2,500 feet, to an opening into Serpent Hall, completely beyond the region of the lakes and rivers. The passage was formerly so very narrow as to be impracticable for public use. But by ingenious engineering, widening certain crevices, and building stairways of stone where needed, blasting away projecting rocks, etc., not only have several interesting rooms been made accessible, but what is far more important, a way of exit has been secured from the remoter parts of the cave in case of a sudden rise in the subterranean streams.

There is also another way out from the Wooden Bowl Room, by a stairway on the right, bearing the whimsical name of the Steeps of Time. Down this we go to a lower level, and proceed along the Arched Way, leading to a wonderful region of pits and domes. Early writers mention the finding of moccason tracks near a basin here called Richardson's Spring, where every body stops for a taste of the clear water flowing down from the rocks. Plodding quietly along for 150 yards, the guide suddenly cries, "Danger on the right!" Beside our path yawns a chasm called the Side-saddle Pit, from the shape of a projecting rock, on which we seat ourselves, and watch with fearful interest the rolls of oiled paper lighted by the guide and dropped into the abyss. Down they go in a fiery spiral, burning long enough to give us a view of its corrugated sides and of a mass of blackened sticks and timbers sixty-five feet below, the distance being thus measured by a line and plummet. The opening is twenty-five feet across, and above it, or nearly so, is Minerva's Dome, thirty-five feet high.

Descending a stairway, 50 yards beyond, we enter the Labyrinth,* a narrow, winding passage, barely wide enough for two persons to go abreast; and after climbing a second stairway and going down a third, and turning about till we are almost bewildered, we find ourselves peering through a window-like aperture into profound darkness. The gloom is intensified by the monotonous sound of dripping water that seems to fall from a vast height to a dis-

---

*The original Labyrinth was near Crocodilopolis (Arsinoe), not far from the Lake Mœris, in Egypt. Herodotus describes it as "consisting of 1,500 chambers excavated under ground, and as many above the surface, the whole inclosed by a wall." He explored a number of the mazes. No traces of it now exist. Perhaps filled up with sand. A second labyrinth was made in Tuscany, a third in Lemnos, and a fourth in Crete.

"As the Cretan labyrinth of old
With wandering ways, and many a winding fold,
Involved the weary feet without redress,
In a round error which denied recess."—(*Virgil's Æneid.*)

mal depth. The guide bids us stay where we are, while he
goes to a smaller window still further on, through which
he thrusts blue lights and blazing rolls, disclosing inde-
scribable wonders to our gaze. Igniting magnesium (of
which it is well to have a supply, as it is not furnished by
the guides), we discern the floor far below us, about an
acre in area, its general level about 90 feet lower than the
window. A small pit in it leads to a body of water 12
feet deep, making the total distance to the lowest point
117 feet. The height of the vault over-head seems to be
about 100 feet; which gives 217 feet as the extreme alti-
tude of this mighty chasm known as Gorin's Dome. It
used to be called 500 feet high; but as the distance from the
surface to drainage level is now known to be only 328 feet,
that fact effectually disposes of such exaggerated estimates.
The perpendicular walls are draped with three immense
stalagmitic curtains, one above another, whose folds,
which seem to be loosely floating, are bordered with fringes
rich and heavy. These hangings, dight with figures rare
and fantastic, fit for Plutonian halls, were woven in Nature's loom by crystal threads of running water!

Putnam's Cabinet, and Hovey's Cabinet, still further on
in the Labyrinth, are smaller domes, where concretions
known as cave-pearls, are found, and also some of the
finest alabaster in the cave. Here, too, are specimens of
oölitic limestone, which under the microscope has the appearance of being made up of tiny eggs. The passage
terminates in Ariadne's Grotto.

On retracing our way out of the Labyrinth, we next
come to the famous abyss known as the Bottomless Pit,
above which expands Shelby's Dome. This frightful pit
was long regarded as constituting an impassable barrier to
further progress; but its terrors have been greatly over-
drawn. The author of "Warwick, or the Lost National-
ities of America," makes his hero descend *many miles* into
the Bottomless Pit, by the aid of Stephen the guide! The
depth of the chasm has ordinarily been given as more than
200 feet. It is really a double pit, being nearly divided
by a tongue of rock that juts into it for 27 feet; from the

point of which, in 1837. Stephen threw a ladder across, and ventured into the unknown regions beyond. A substantial bridge now spans the gulf, which, for safety is renewed every four years. Leaning over the hand-rails, we safely admire the gleaming rolls as they whirl to and fro, slowly sinking till they vanish, lighting up, in their capricious progress, the wrinkles and furrows made by the torrent's flow during untold ages. Bringing the mysterious abyss to the severe test of line and plummet, we find its depth to be, on one side only 95 feet, and on the other 105 feet. Shelby's Dome overhead may be 60 feet high, and the space between 15 feet, thus making 180 feet the greatest distance from top to bottom of the entire chasm.

Reveler's Hall, the first room beyond the Bottomless Pit, is about 40 feet in diameter and 20 feet high, and was formerly a place where parties stopped to dine. The path to our left leads to the Rivers, which are reserved for another time. That on the right is Pensico Avenue, about a mile long, and containing various objects of interest. The Sea Turtle is the first of these to which our attention is called; a rock fallen from the roof and shaped like the carapace of a huge tortoise, 30 feet in diameter. Wild Hall is next entered, where the great rocks are strewn about in the most amazing disorder, under a roof of elaborate lancet arches. A low passage on the left, called Bunyan's Way, communicates with River Hall, but is seldom traversed, as visitors take the more direct path mentioned above. Proceeding still through Pensico Avenue, we admire the snowy nodules incrusting the Snowball Arch, beneath which we go on to the Grand Crossings, where four avenues meet. This place is much admired. The same is true of Mat's Arcade, 50 yards long, 30 feet wide and 60 high, where Mat himself pointed out to us the series of cavern floors that had successively given way leaving four narrow terraces along the entire length of the walls. A large white column is called, for some unknown reason, the Pine-Apple Bush. A little beyond this formation is the Hanging Grove, where the stalactites resemble branches of coral rather than those of trees. About a hundred yards on and we arrive at Angelica's Grotto, sparkling with crystals.

This is the end of the Short Route; and here this chapter might also end, were it not that I wish to describe certain remarkable pits discovered, in February 1881, by Mr. J. T. Hill and William Garvin the guide. These are not ordinarily exhibited, on account of their dangerous surroundings; and, indeed, I was assured that I was the first visitor who had been permitted to explore the locality, though it had been seen by several persons connected with the Cave.

The approach is by a low, creeping passage, opening from the Arched Way, and leading across what has for many years been known only to be shunned—the Covered Pit. This treacherous chasm is imperfectly concealed by loose slabs of limestone, between which the black depths seem to be lying in wait for the heedless explorer. Cautiously crossing it, and crawling on our hands and knees for some distance further, we stopped, and William told me to listen to the slow dripping of a waterfall. Throwing a pebble in the direction of the sound, I could hear it bound from side to side as it descended, until, after a long interval, it fell into a body of water below. On examination we found that we lay on a rocky partition between the old Covered Pit on the right, and a new one on the left. The latter proved to be a pit within a pit, as we found on throwing lighted paper down its mouth. The upper one is about 90 feet deep, and at its bottom we could just discern the orifice of the lower one.

I was anxious to find a point from which to examine this inner pit to better advantage. Creeping back from off the partition, we made our way around a rocky pillar for perhaps 40 yards, and came upon the further edge of the pit that had excited our curiosity, and also found another horrible pit on the left, separated from the first by a ridge only six feet wide! The proximity of the two chasms suggested to Mr. Klett the names of Scylla for the first, and Charybdis for the second; in memory of the classic line :

" Incidis in Scyllam cupiens vitare Charybdim."

(You may fall into Scylla, trying to shun Charybdis.)

Willing to run some risk to accomplish my object, I clambered a short distance down into Scylla, to a ledge overhanging its very deepest portion, and cleft by a serpentine crevice about five inches wide. Dropping pebbles through this crack, we timed them as they fell unobstructed, and by repeated trials found the time taken in reaching the bottom to be exactly five seconds by the watch. This, by a well-known formula for calculating accelerated motion, would give 402 feet as the depth *in vacuo.* Making due allowance for the resistance of the atmosphere, and for the time necessary for the sound to return, the space passed was not less than 200, nor more than 250 feet. William, not satisfied with scientific guess-work, produced his ball of cord, fastened a lamp to its end, and let it down into the darkness. The glimmering light served to show the irregular walls of the abyss, as it descended, until at length it caught on a projecting rock. In his efforts to shake it loose, the cord was burned off; but the lamp remained where it had lodged, shining on as if determined to do its duty to the last! The part of the cord that was drawn up measured 135 feet, leaving us, after all, to conjecture the remaining depth. Probably the pit perforates the limestone down to the drainage level—a distance according to the barometer, of 220 feet.

Glad to forsake the thin crust on which we stood, overhanging such prodigious depths, we climbed out of the jaws of Scylla, and made experiments on Charybdis. Here, again, the pebbles were five seconds in reaching the pool below. Along the perilous rim William led the way to still another chasm, which we identified as the farther edge of the Bottomless Pit. Regaining, not without some difficulty, the bridge over it, we proceeded a short distance on the path that leads to River Hall, and then turned back, by a passage under the rocks, to an opening into the side of the Bottomless Pit, about 40 feet below the bridge.

Here we saw the famous pit in a new light, and also obtained the best view to be had of Shelby's Dome. The accompanying picture of the Bottomless Pit was taken from this point of view. While we were standing there, on the occasion referred to, I noticed a volume of smoke issuing from a window beyond us. Investigating this phenomenon, we found ourselves looking again into Charybdis, though not at its deepest part. The smoke came from the blue lights we had ignited just before leaving it.

Thus, as we have shown, there are, within an a r e a whose d i a m e t e r does not perhaps exceed 600 yards, six of the largest naturally formed pits in the known world, besides several others of smaller dimensions; and the entire group is joined together by connecting p a s s - ages. An inspection of the accompanying diagram

THE BOTTOMLESS PIT.

(opposite page 45) will enable the reader to get an idea of this extraordinary locality.

On inquiring of Mr. Klett if there was any sink-hole in the vicinity to correspond with this cluster of chasms,

he directed me to a piece of unbroken forest, less than half a mile from the Mammoth Cave Hotel, where all the requirements of the case seem to be met. This vast depression embraces many acres, and is so deep that, when standing on its edge, one can overlook the tops of the trees growing in the central portion. It remains to be proved by further explorations whether there are any hidden tunnels of communication between it and the remarkable group of domes and pits I have been trying to describe.

A SNOW CLOUD. (See page 59.)

CHAPTER V.

MAMMOTH CAVE has gained a reputation as a cave of "magnificent distances;" and many a critical visitor has set himself to correct the over-estimates of others. Yet the fact remains that the Long Route is a day's journey under ground. The signal for starting is given at 9 A. M., and the return is about 6 P. M., after nine hours of steady walking over a road, a little rough in spots, but for the most part quite smooth and easy. I was one of "a rapid transit party," one day, that tried to see how quickly the trip could be made. None but fast walkers were included, and no stops were made, except at points of special interest; and the time consumed was just seven hours. Allowing, therefore, two miles an hour as the rate of travel, it follows that the Long Route is not less than 14 miles, nor more than 18; and this estimate may as well be accepted until the distance is exactly measured. Long as the trip is few persons find it fatiguing, being sustained by the variety and novelty of the scenery, and also by the cool and pure air for which the cave is celebrated.

Down the valley again, and under the thick horizontal plates of limestone, from whose green and mossy ledge the wild pattering rill falls on the rocks below ; on through the

Narrows, and the Rotunda, where perhaps a generation of dead men sleep; climbing the piles left by the niter-diggers of old, or led by the musical ringing of the guide's footsteps on the hard rocky floor; between heavy buttresses bending beneath the gray ceiling above, or walls hollowed into low-browed niches and nobler arches—thus we go through the wide and lofty Main Cave until the Giant's Coffin is reached. This rock was originally christened the "Steamboat," and the early accounts explained the points of resemblance, and had poetical things to say about her "reposing in her river of stone." Creeping around her bows, we next descend into those dens of darkness, the Deserted Chambers, and soon hear the faithful guide call out 'danger on the right!" Safely by the terrible pits, we pause to take breath, meanwhile blowing our lights out in order to prove by the "horror of a great darkness" what a blessed thing light is. Happy are we in the knowledge that the lamps are still near, and our pockets full of matches! A brief imprisonment in an atmosphere that seems to have been suddenly solidified to a mass of coal suffices, and we relight our lamps and march on.

"March," however, is not just the right word; for progress now is by the Valley of Humility, a low passage four feet high, conducting us into the Scotchman's Trap, where a canny Scot paused lest the broad rock, suspended by the tip, might fall and bury those venturing through the circular orifice beneath. Less timid than he, we dive down the trap-door, and presently are made acquainted with the famous and original Fat Man's Misery, of which all others are but base imitations. Some fastidious soul once tried to change this name to "the Winding Way," but the attempt was a failure. Here the path enters a serpentine channel, whose walls, 18 inches apart, change direction 8 times in 236 feet, while the average distance from the sandy floor to the ledge overhead is but 5 feet. The rocky sides are beautifully marked with waves and ripples, as if running water had been suddenly petrified. There seems to have been first a horizontal opening between two strata, by taking advantage of which this singular channel was chiseled, from whose too close embrace we gladly emerge into Great Relief, where we can straighten our spines, and enjoy once more the luxury of taking a full breath. The question is sometimes asked, "How fat a man is the fattest man that can get through the Fat Man's Misery?" Some reader may be comforted by learning that, in August, 1881, Mr. Abraham Menks, a colored man from Lebanon, Ky., whose weight was previously 282½ pounds, succeeded in the attempt. He did without help till he came to the place where the floor comes up and the roof comes down, to bother tall men as well as fat ones, and then William, who is equal to any emergency, helped him through.

"How did you manage it?" said a listener to the story, as it was told at the hotel that evening.

"Easy enough," gravely answered the guide. "I took him through in sections." Menks himself claimed to have lost 15 pounds in the operation, and the guides, to this day, point out places where the rocks had to bend to let this jolly fat man through!

It was formerly supposed that if this passage were blocked up, escape from the regions beyond would be impossible. But another mode of exit was discovered by William, in 1871, through the Cork-screw. This intricate web of fissures was known as long ago as 1837, but not as a passage through to River Hall. In the oldest published accounts of Mammoth Cave it is stated that "among the Kentucky Cliffs, just under the ceiling, is a gap in the wall, into which you can scramble, and make your way down a chaotic gulf, creeping like a rat under and among huge loose rocks, to a depth of 80 or 90 feet—provided you do not break your neck before you get half way." Since William made his way through, the obstructions have partly been removed, so that now, by mounting three stairways, crawling through narrow crevices, and leaping from rock to rock, one may ascend for what would perhaps be a vertical distance of 150 feet, and thus reduce the journey from the mouth of the cave to Great Relief by

nearly a mile. Visitors who come in one way, generally
go out the other, and regard the last route chosen the
worst, whichever it may have been.

The guide calls attention, as we now proceed, to the
Odd Fellow's Links, and other concretions on the ceiling,
which are caused by the wearing away of the more soluble
limestone from around hard ridges of ironstone, leaving
these emblems in bass-relief.

Bacon Chamber is a still more striking instance of mimickry, for the masses of rock projecting from the ceiling
certainly look like the rows of hams in a packing-house,
and it seems as if nature must have made this chamber
when in some jocose mood.

Spark's Avenue runs from the Bacon Chamber to the
Mammoth Dome, the most spacious of the many domes in
this cave. As this is a "special route," I took my guide
early one morning, long before the regular hour for parties to enter for the Long Route, meaning to complete the
trip in time to join a large company of tourists from Nashville, who were going beyond the rivers. My guide, on
this occasion, was Tom Lee, and we were accompanied by
Barton, the artist, whose pencil has furnished many of the
cuts that embellish this volume. Leaving the latter to
make a drawing of the Cork-screw, Tom and I entered
Sparks' Avenue, which, as he told me, is named for Mr.
C. A. Sparks, of New York. It begins well by an ample
room named Bandit's Hall, where there is a wild confusion of huge rocks. Brigg's Avenue, to the right of it, we
did not explore, though it is said to be of great extent. I
also took for granted the "petrified saw-logs" in Clarissa's
Dome, at the end of Sylvan Avenue. 100 yards on our left,
after leaving Newman's Spine—a crevice where we have
the privilege of straightening our own spines, after no little stooping. We finally emerged from Sparks' Avenue,
and found ourselves on a terrace thirty feet long and fifteen feet wide, confronted by a realm of empty darkness.
Our lamps revealed neither floor, nor roof, nor opposite
wall. And this is Mammoth Dome, the grandest hall in
all this domain of silence and of night. I directed Tom to

leave me here, and to return for my comrade and for fire-
works.

Not until Tom's glittering light was gone, and his retreating steps had ceased to echo along the corridor, did I
realize the utter loneliness that surrounded me. I sat on
the edge of the terrace for a time, and amused myself by
throwing lighted papers down, thus discovering that the
floor was less than forty feet below me, and was accessible
only by a rude ladder blackened with age. Here and
there a rung was missing, and I hesitated to trust myself
to such a fragile support. Retreating into the avenue, I
whiled the time away by catching cave crickets, till Tom
and Barton came with twenty lamps and a supply of red
fire and bengolas.

Carefully descending the treacherous ladder, which has
since been replaced by a substantial stairway, we lighted
up the huge dome, by burning magnesium at three points
at once, and estimated its dimensions to be about 400 feet
in length, 150 feet in width, and varying from 80 to 250
feet in height. The floor slopes down to a pool that receives a waterfall from the summit of the dome. The
walls are curtained by alabaster drapery in vertical folds,
varying in size from a pipe-stem to a saw-log, and deco-
rated by heavy fringes at intervals of about twenty feet.
A huge gateway at the farther end of the hall, opens into
a room so like the ruins of Luxor and Karnak, that we
named it the Egyptian Temple. The floor here is paved
with stalagmitic blocks, stained by red and black oxides
into a kind of mosaic. Six colossal columns, 80 feet
from base to capital, and 25 feet in diameter, stand
in a semi-circle, flanked by pyramidal towers. The material of the shafts is gray oolite, fluted by deep furrows, with sharp ridges between : the whole column being
veneered with yellow stalagmite, rich as jasper, and covered by tracery as elaborate as Chinese carving. The cap-
itals are projecting slabs of limestone, and the bases are
garnished by mushroom-shaped stalagmites. The largest
of them is Caliban's Cushion. By an opening behind the
third column in the row, we clambered down a steep de-

scent into gloomy catacombs beneath, which we did not fully explore for lack of time. Tom pointed out to us, on our way back to the terrace, an opening overhead, and assured us that it was identical with the Crevice Pit in the branch of Audubon's Avenue, known as the Little Bat Room.

In old times the miners, in searching for the best beds of saltpeter-earth, had the notion that there must be a very rich deposit in the Crevice Pit, and one of them, in examining it, dropped his lamp. He climbed down into the ugly black hole, and tried to get his lamp again by feeling around with a stick. Suddenly the stick fell rattling down an abyss.

THE EGYPTIAN TEMPLE.

A sprightly young negro volunteered to be let down at the end of a rope, as a sort of animated plummet, to sound the depth of the pit. The story he told, on being drawn up again, was so wonderful that nobody believed him, of a spacious and splendid room, far larger than the Rotunda. When Mr. Edmund F. Lee, a civil engineer of Cincinnati, made his survey of Mammoth Cave, in 1835, he tied a stone to a string and "struck bottom at 280 feet." As the real distance is less than 100 feet, the probability is that he paid out the rope after the stone rested; or else that the stone rolled down toward the pool below, and was then drawn up and the whole length of cord taken as telling the depth.

One of the guides named John Buford, while accompanying a certain visitor named Smith, in 1843, discovered the entrance through Sparks' Avenue, to the immense room that was named, in honor of the explorer, "Smith's Mammoth Dome." On a subsequent visit, one of the guides—I think it was old Mat—found the miner's lamp lying on the floor where it had fallen thirty years before.

It was time to return, if we were to carry out our original plan. On the way, Tom called our attention to certain signs on the walls, by means of which the guides could tell their way, if they were at any time in doubt. Each guide has his own mark, and it is said that many a time, when one of the later ones has congratulated himself on a new discovery, he has been chagrined by finding Stephen's or Mat's sign on the wall, showing a previous visit.

On entering River Hall, we followed a path skirting the edge of cliffs sixty feet high and one hundred feet long, embracing the sullen waters to which the name of Dead Sea is given. Descending a flight of steps, we came to a cascade, but a little further on, by some conjectured to be a reappearance of the waterfall at the entrance of the cave. It precipitates itself into a funnel-shaped hollow in a massive mud-bank. On another visit, in 1881, we found a natural bed of mushrooms growing here, a species of Agaricus, that has suggested the idea of a mushroom farm, similar to those at Frépilon and Méry, in France, whence many thousands of bushels are sent to market annually. It is laid out in Audubon Avenue.

Our various speculations were broken in upon by the hilarious sounds heralding the party under Mat's escort, long before they came in view. There never was a prettier sight than this merry company, sixty in all, as with flashing lamps and spangled costumes they skirted the somber terrace, astonishing the gnomes by "Litoria," and other jolly college songs. They wound past us, in single file, disappearing behind a wall of stone to come into view again on the natural bridge, whence they swung their lamps to catch sight of the River Stix, on whose banks we now were standing.

The estimated length of the Styx is 400 feet, and its breadth about 40 feet. It was formerly crossed by boat, before the discovery of the natural bridge, whence Mat's party are hailing us with invitations to join their number and go on.

CROSSING THE STYX.

Lake Lethe comes next—a body of water about as large as the Styx, and, like it, once crossed only by boat. It is now lower than formerly, being slowly filled with mud, and a narrow path runs along its margin, at the foot of cliffs 90 feet high, leading to a pontoon at the neck of the lake. Crossing this, we step upon a beach of the finest yellow sand. This is the Great Walk, extending to Echo river, a distance of 500 yards, under a lofty ceiling mottled

with white and black limestones, like snow-clouds drifting
in a wintry sky. A rise of only five feet would completely
cover this sandy walk, and this is its condition for from
four to eight months in every year. The streams are
usually low in summer, when there are also the most visitors—a fortunate coincidence.

The connection of the cave rivers with Green river has
been demonstrated by the simple experiment of throwing
chaff upon them, which comes to the surface in the upper
and lower big springs; deep, bubbling pools, lying half a
mile apart, under cliffs bristling with hemlock and pine.
When these pools are submerged by a freshet in Green
river, the streams in the cave are united into a continuous
body of water. The rise is augmented by the torrents
emptied down through the sink-holes, and sometimes is so
great as to touch the iron railing above the Dead Sea.

The subsidence of so vast a body of water, although for
some reason less rapid than of streams without, must be
with powerful suction causing eddies and whirlpools. In
order to save from destruction, at such times, the uncouth
little fleet, built of planks and timbers, every piece of
which was brought in through passes we had traversed
with difficulty empty-handed, the boats are securely fastened, when not in use, by long ropes or twisted grape-
vines that let them swim with the flood.

The first persons that ever crossed the rivers were
Stephen, the guide, with Mr. John Craig, of Philadelphia,
and Mr. Brice Patton, a teacher in the Blind Asylum at
Louisville. A number of blind men and women have, at
different times, visited Mammoth Cave. Mat piloted four
in one party in 1880. They took only the Short Route.
They seemed much interested, and talked about what they
had *seen*, and said that every thing was very fine!

Four boats now await us on the banks of Echo river.
Each has seats on the gunwales for twenty passengers,
while the guide stands in the bow and propels the primitive craft by a long paddle, or by grasping projecting
rocks. There is hardly a perceptible current at any season when the stream can be crossed at all; hence the inac-

curacy of pictures that represent the river as boisterous,
and frantic oarsmen striving with might and main to keep
the boat from shipwreck. And as the only gale in the
entire cavern is that which blows *out* of its mouth, there
is equal impropriety in a striking picture I have seen of
sail-boats on this unruffled tide!

The low arch, only three or four feet high, under which
we go at embarkation, soon rises to a height varying from
ten to thirty feet, while the plummet shows a still greater
depth below. The surface at low water is by the barometer but 20 feet above the level of Green river; and this
may, therefore be regarded as the lowest part of the cave,
at least so far as it is accessible to visitors.*

The width of Echo River varies from 20 to 200 feet, and
its length is said to be about three quarters of a mile.
Throughout its entire extent there are only one or two
points where a landing could be made, and the stream can
not properly be said to have any shore. Hence the guides
exercise the strictest authority, in order to guard against
accidents.

Matt secures for our exclusive use a boat smaller than
those into which the others crowd. He then draws from
a hiding-place a hand-net, and tries to catch for us a few
of the famous eyeless fish, that dart to and fro, but vanish
on the least agitation of the waters. His success at this
time was not very encouraging. But subsequently, on
other trips, we captured numerous specimens, from two to
six inches long, and usually destitute even of rudimentary
organs of vision. Several, however, had protuberances or
sightless eyes, and one had good eye-sight. The grada-
tions of color are from olive-brown to pure white; while
some are perfectly transparent. They have simple cartilage instead of bones, and are destitute of scales. They
are known to be viviparous, the young being born in October, and without external eyes when born. There are
also blind and white crawfish, that are oviparous, as is
proved by a fine specimen now in my cabinet, which still

*One authority makes the river 240 feet below the mouth of the
cave, by barometric measurement. Others make it but 174 feet.

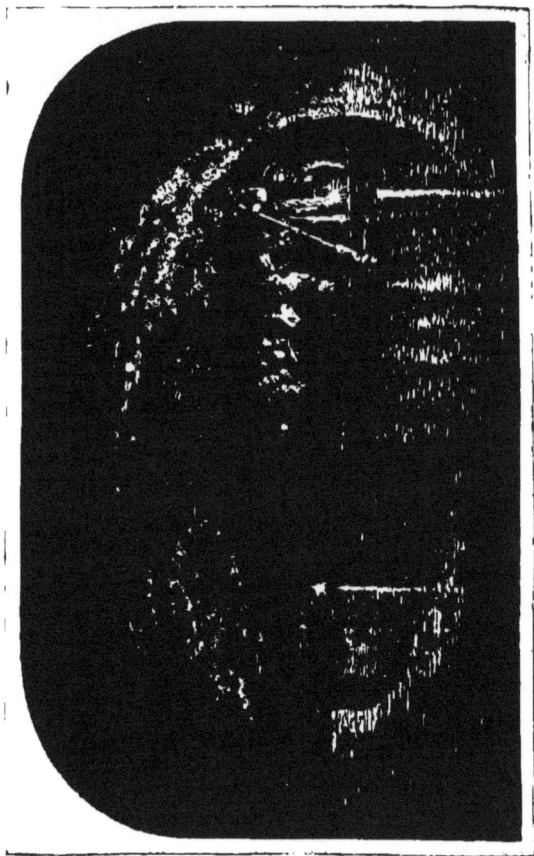

Boat Ride on Echo River.

carries its cluster of salmon-colored eggs. The Cambarus and Amblyopsis have a wide distribution: being found in many other caves, and also in certain deep wells, both in Kentucky and in Indiana. These, as well as other true subterranean fauna, may be regarded as chiefly of Pleistocene origin; yet certain forms are supposed to be remnants of Tertiary, and possibly of Cretaceous life. The strongly marked divergence of cave-animals from those found outside, convinced the elder Agassiz that they were especially created for the limits within which they dwell. But it is doubtful if there is more variability than can be accounted for by their migration, many generations ago, from the outer world to a realm of absolute silence and perpetual darkness.

Along the water's edge are cavities, from a few inches to many feet in depth, washed out by the stream. These gave a wag along with the jolly Nashville party an opportunity to break the silence that had settled over the voyagers, and he shouted with absurd glee, pointing to the cavities :

"Oh, see these little bits o' caves—three for five cents!"

The solemn echoes caught his silly tones, and bore them, as if in derision, hither and thither and far away. When the peals of laughter that followed had died away, a quiet lady in black velvet led the company in sacred song. The concord of sweet sounds was surprisingly agreeable.

Allowing the Nashville party to go on without us, we remained alone on Echo river, floating over its strangely transparent water, as if gliding through the air, and trying every echo its arches were capable of producing. A single aerial vibration given with energy, as by a pistol-shot, rebounded from rock to rock. The din awakened by discordant sounds was frightful. On the other hand when the voice gave the tones of a full chord *seriatim*, they came back in a sweeping *arpeggio*. Flute-music produced charming reverberations; and the cornet still finer effects. It should be explained that this symmetrical passage-way does not give back a distinct *echo*, as the term is commonly used, but a harmonious prolongation of sound for from 10 to 30 seconds after the original impulse. The long vault has a certain key-note of its own, which, when firmly struck, excites harmonics including tones of incredible depth and sweetness, reminding me of the profound undertone one hears in the music of Niagara Falls.

An extraordinary result was obtained by the guide's agitating the water vigorously with his broad paddle, and then seating himself in silence by my side. The first sound that broke the stillness was like the tinkling of silver bells. Larger and heavier bells then seemed to take up the melody, as the waves sought out the cavities in the rock. And then it appeared as if all chimes of all cathedrals had conspired to raise a tempest of sweet sounds. They then died away to utter silence. We still sat in expectation. Lo, as if from some deep recess that had been hitherto forgotten, came a tone tender and profound; after which, like gentle memories, were re-awakened all the mellow sounds that had gone before, until River Hall rang again. Those who try their own voices are pleased to have the hollow wall give back shout and song, whimsical cry and merry peal; but the nymphs reserve their choicest harmonies for those who are willing to listen in silence to the voice of many waters.

A rocky inlet receives our craft, and as we land we are greeted by the melody of a cascade that breaks itself into pearls on the sloping ledges. An avenue extends from Cascade Hall to Roaring river—a succession of shallow ripples and deep basins, navigated by a canoe. The passage-way through which it flows has an echo of remarkable power, but hoarse rather than musical.

We overtake Mat's party in Silliman's Avenue, where the irregular floor, rugged walls finished by a well marked cornice, and sides pierced by cavities, show that we are now in a portion of recent formation as compared with the Main Cave. Among points of interest in this long avenue, may be mentioned the Dripping Spring, around which are grouped the first stalactites we have seen since entering River Hall. The scarcity of these ornaments in a cave so large as this has often excited remark. The explanation probably is, that the massive limestone from which it is excavated is almost completely covered by a bed of sandstone, through which the water makes its way, not by percolation, but through fissures and sink-holes. Hence the present dryness of large portions of the cave, and their lack of stalactites. The Infernal Region is the odious name given to a miserably wet and disagreeable spot beyond the Spring, and it does not surprise us to have Serpent Hall come next, where the guide points out the trail of the reptile on the wall overhead. Here also is the inner terminus of the Ganter Avenue, that leads by a dry path back to the Main Cave. In a side-cut called the Valley Way, we find white masses of fibrous gypsum. Beyond the Hill of Fatigue stands the Great Western, like the stern of an immense ship, with its rudder to the starboard. We mount to a slender ledge between the Vale of Flowers and Rabbit-rock, and follow Rhoda's Arcade for 500 yards, amid rare incrustations, to twin-domes, seldom visited because so difficult of access. The one we enter is about 60 feet in diameter, and opens into the other by a gothic window 150 feet above the floor. The guide climbs up to it, and burns magnesium, while we do the same below. Thus we are enabled to survey the long stalagmitic curtains that drape the sides, and to catch a glimpse of the oval apex, 300 feet over us. This is Lucy's Dome—the loftiest natural dome yet discovered!

Silliman's Avenue (named for Prof. Silliman, of Yale College), ends in Ole Bull's Concert Hall, where the renowned violinist once gave a musical entertainment.

Continuing our journey by a picturesque pass, known as El Ghor, we have successively brought to notice, the Fly Chamber, whose walls are singularly sprinkled with little crystals of black gypsum; Suicide Rock, so-called "because it hung itself;" Table Rock or the Sheep-shelter; the Crown, and other curiosities. Corinna's Dome, 9 feet wide and 40 high, rests directly over El Ghor; the Black Hole of Calcutta, is an ugly pit on the left of the pass; while a narrow avenue further on leads to Stella's Dome,

250 feet high, and said to be very fine, though rarely visited.

El Ghor may be followed half a mile further, and is said to communicate with Mystic River—on what authority I do not know, for none of the guides could give information concerning it. We leave the gorge at a small basin called Hebe's Spring, by climbing by a ladder up 20 feet, and going, one at a time, through a very uninviting hole in the roof; and thus we gain admittance to an upper tier of caverns. When the last man is through by burning magnesium, we are surprised to find ourselves in a vineyard—the famous Mary's (or Martha's) Vineyard! Countless nodules and globules simulate clusters on clusters of luscious grapes, burdening hundreds of boughs and gleaming with party-colored tints through the dripping dew. No covetous hand is permitted to gather this marvelous vintage. By a detour one may reach a natural chapel, named by an enraptured priest, the Holy Sepulcher; there are fine stalactites also in the vicinity.

Leaving this enchanted ground we soon enter Washington Hall, which is but a smoke-stained lunch-room, strewn with relics of hundreds of dining-parties, while along its walls are the sharp fragments of numberless bottles that have survived their usefulness. We find that servants from the hotel have anticipated our coming, and have spread for us an abundant meal. Vigorous exercise whets the appetite, and we leave but few remnants for the rats. Cans of oil are kept here, and while we dine the guides trim and fill the lamps.

The ceiling of the next room is dotted with hemispherical masses of snowy gypsum, each of which is from 2 to 10 inches in diameter, looking like snow-balls hurled against the wall and sticking there.

A charming special trip is from this point down Marion Avenue, said to be a mile and a half long. It is from 20 to 60 feet wide, has a clean, sandy floor, and a clouded ceiling. At its farther end it has two branches. That on the left leads to Zoe's Grotto. The other branch leads to

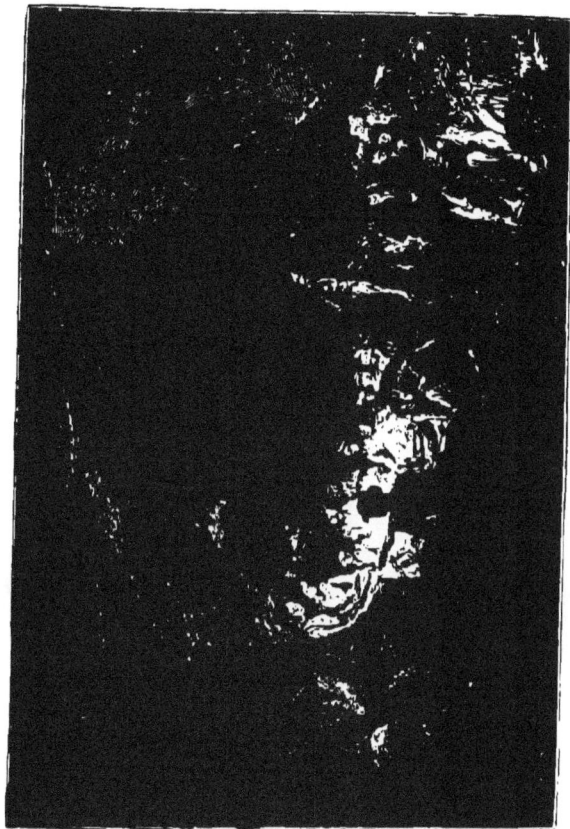

Dinner in the Shade.

a Paradise where all the flowers are fair and crystalline, and which, in the opinion of some of the guides, is the most beautiful place in the whole cave. Portia's Parterre is of the same general description; while Digby's Dome is remarkable simply because it cuts through to the sandstone.

The regular route takes us, however, next into that treasure-house of alabaster brilliants known as Cleveland's Cabinet. What words can picture forth its beauty? Imagine symmetrical arches, of 50 feet span, where the fancy is at once enlivened and bewildered by a mimickry of every flower that grows in the garden, forest, or prairie, from the modest daisy to the flaunting helianthus.

Select, for examination, a single one of these cave flowers—the "oulopholites" of the mineralogist. Consider the charms of this queenly rose that has unfolded its petals in Mary's Bower. From a central stem gracefully curl countless crystals, fibrous and pellucid; each tiny crystal is in itself a study; each fascicle of curved prisms is wonderful; and the whole blossom is a miracle of beauty.

Now multiply this mimic flower from one to a hundred, a thousand, a myriad. Move down the dazzling vista, as if in a dream of Elysium—not for a few yards, or rods, but for one or two miles! All is virgin white, except here and there a little patch of gray limestone, or a spot bronzed by some metallic stain, or again, as we purposely vary the lovely monotony by burning colored lights. Midway is a great floral cross overhead, formed by the natural grouping of stone rosettes. Floral clusters, bouquets, wreaths, garlands, embellish nearly every foot of the ceiling and walls; and the very soil sparkles with trodden jewels. The pendulous fringes of the night-blooming cereus are rivaled by the snowy plumes that float from rifts and crevices, forever safe from the withering glare of day-light. Clumps of lilies, pale pansies, blanched tulips, drooping fuchsias, sprays of asters, spikes of tube-roses, wax-leaved magnolias,—but why exhaust the botanical catalogue? The fancy finds every gem of the green-house and parterre in this crystalline conservatory. Earlier visitors have described long sprays, like stalks of celery, run-

ning vines, and branches of a chandelier, and I had not
believed them. But when I told my doubts to good old
Mat, he kindly took me to a spot where they were still to
be seen—in Charlotte's Grotto. It has been impossible to
guard all these exquisite formations from covetous fingers,
and too many have been smoked by the lamps of careless
visitors. But happily the subtle forces of nature are at
work to mend what man has marred, and to replace by
fresh creations what has gone to the mineralogist's cabinet
or the amateur's *étagère.*

Cleveland's Cabinet terminates at the base of a pile of
fragments fallen from the roof, and dignified by the name
of the Rocky Mountains. Its height does not exceed 100
feet, and the gorge the other side of it, the Dismal Hollow,
is only about 70 feet deep.

The cave here divides into three branches. That on the
right leads a long distance, and ends in Sandstone Dome,
the roof of which, judging from its material, can not be far
below the surface. The middle branch is named Franklin
Avenue, from 30 to 60 feet wide, and about a quarter of a
mile long. The path is very uneven and wild. It leads
to a circular canopy 12 feet in diameter, called Serena's
Arbor, thus described by a clerical writer in the New
York Observer: "It is, of itself, floor, sides, roof, and
ornaments, one perfect, seamless, stalactite, of a beautiful
hue and exquisite workmanship. Folds or blades of stalactitic matter hang like drapery around the sides, reaching half way down to the floor; and opposite the door, a
canopy of stone projects, elegantly ornamented, as if it
were the resting-place of a fairy bride."

Tourists generally are content with taking the left-hand
path, which leads them at once to Croghan's Hall, which
is the end of the Long Route. This hall is about 60 feet
in diameter, and 35 feet high, and contains the finest stalactites in the cave, many of them, however, sadly disfig-
ured. Some of them are translucent and very hard. On
the right is the Maelstrom, a pit 20 feet wide, and said to
be 175 feet deep. It is due to the memory of a daring
youth to tell how Mr. W. C. Prentice, son of the poet and

editor, George D. Prentice, descended this abyss in quest of adventures.

As the guides tell the story, they furnished a rope by which the young hero was lowered, amid fearful and enchanting scenes, then first lighted since creation's morning by the feeble rays of his solitary lamp. Midway he encountered a waterfall, spouting from the wall, into whose sparkling shower he unavoidably swung. Escaping all dangers, he stood at last on the solid rock below. On his way up, he swung himself into a huge niche, whence he roamed through wide and wondrous chambers till checked by rocky barriers. Then returning to the place where he had fastened his rope to a stalactite, he found it disentangled and dangling beyond his reach. Ingeniously twisting the wires of his lamp into a long hook, he caught hold again, and signaled to the guides to draw him up. It is said (believe it who may) that they did this with such zeal that the cable was fired by friction, and that one of the guides crawled out on the beam and emptied a flask of water on the burning rope! The whole story, with all its embellishments, is done into spirited verse by Rev. George Lansing Taylor. The hero himself, whose life was so miraculously spared, finally sacrificed it during the late war. Prentice has had at least one imitator, if not two, who accomplished the descent into the Maelstrom, but without his adventures.

A dog-story worth telling is connected with the last trip I made to the end of the Long Route, in 1881, as it offers some striking peculiarities. Many a dog will bravely follow his master amid tangled forests and lofty hills, that will refuse to go with him into a dark and silent cave.

Jack, the old house-dog at the hotel, is not an exception to this rule; for he has long had the habit of escorting guests as far as the Iron Gate. There he waits till all have gone in, and then trots home again, his duty done. But Jack has had a companion in his old age.

"We call him *Brigham*," explains William, "'cause he's *Young*, you know!"

From the first Brigham seemed to have no fear of dark-

ness. The two dogs would trot side by side, as far as the
Iron Gate ; but there they would part. Jack would return, as usual, to the hotel; while Brigham would push
on into the cave. The latter grew to be a great favorite
with the guides ; and Manager Klett warned us not to lose
him when we took him in with us.

The day that Brigham went with us on the Long Route,
he grew very weary, and cared less for the lovely arches of
cave flowers than for some cozy nook, where he might
curl down for a nap. Soon after lunch in Washington
Hall he was missing, and did not come at our repeated
calls.

"Perhaps he has gone ahead to Echo river," said I,
"and is waiting for us there."

"Like enough," said William, "I had n't thought of
that."

But no bounding form or joyful bark welcomed our approach. The echoes answered to our calls, as if a thousand voices were crying for Brigham, as well as we ; and
our whistling was repeated, as if all the spirits of the cave
had been let loose for an Æolian concert.

Plainly the dog was lost! William thought Brigham
might track us as far as the river; but that on reaching
the water he would lose the scent and not try to swim
across. Lighting a freshly filled lamp, he set it on a ledge
at the entrance to a passage called Purgatory, by which,
with only a little swimming, the dog might make his way
around the river.

Sadly we returned to the hotel, where the announce-
ment of the loss caused a sensation. Early the next morning a party crossed Echo river, and there they were met
by Brigham, who returned in the boat with them to this
side. Shortly, however, he again disappeared, and was
left to his fate.

Nothing was seen of him all that day. This time, of
deliberate choice, he remained a second night under
ground. The next morning Jack, too, was missing, and
was found at the Iron Gate, exchanging experiences with
Brigham, who was still behind the bars!

The Corkscrew

Our curiosity led us to examine Brigham's tracks. We found that he had followed our trail, step by step, his only guide, of course, being his sense of smell. Thus he had tracked us, over soft mud-banks and mellow nitrous earth, ridges of sand and heaps of stone, from Echo river to the Corkscrew, by many a spot where a single misstep would have sent the poor lonely creature plunging downward in darkness to inevitable death. On reaching the Corkscrew he did not seem to have hesitated an instant, but climbed up through that intricate and hazardous pass, where most men would be in confusion even with a lamp and a map of the cave. I could not learn that the dog had ever been that way before; and when he went in with us he entered by the way of the Deserted Chambers.

By contrast with this perfect and fearless operation of instinct (which Prof. Brewer cites as a case of "orientation"), the story may be told of Old Mat's escape under somewhat similar circumstances.

Once, during troublous times, Old Mat was at work near the pits when he heard some young men coming with song and with shout, as if they had been taking more wine than was for their good. The ex-slave thought that "discretion was the better part of valor," and hid in a crevice, put his lamp out, and quietly waited for the revelers to pass by. On coming forth from his hiding-place he found that he had no matches, and therefore could not re-light his lamp.

The hour was late, and he feared lest a long time might elapse before help should come; he therefore determined to make his way out in the dark. Feeling cautiously along with his staff, he went safely until it suddenly dropped into a pit of unknown depth. Brave as Mat is known to be, he fell in a swoon, and lay, no one knows how long, on the edge of the chasm. On coming to, he collected his wits as well as he could, and felt with his hands for the path. He presently found it, and proceeded on his perilous journey, making his way finally to the surface. Old Mat told me this story himself, as he and Brig-

ham and I sat on the brink of the very abyss in which he
so narrowly escaped finding a tomb.

The full moon was riding in a cloudless sky, when we
emerged from our last day's journey in the great cavern.
We had, as usual, a practical proof of the purity of the
exhilarating cave atmosphere, by its contrast with that of
the outer world, which seemed heavy and suffocating.
The odors of trees, grass, weeds and flowers were strangely intensified and over-powering. The result of a too sudden transition is frequently faintness and vertigo. The
custom is to linger awhile on the threshold, where the
outer and inner airs mingle. Resting thus, on rustic seats,
near the entrance, my companions and I interchanged our
views concerning this wide subterranean realm whose
secrets we had been exploring. Matt said we had tramped
to and fro, in and out, not less than a hundred miles; and
there was none to dispute him! We had gained less defi-
nite knowledge than we had anticipated; and had a surfeit
of conjectures, estimates and mysteries. We were grateful,
however, for the impressions we had received, and for the
memories retained of wonderful scenes and strange adventures. Feelings akin to friendship had sprung up within
us for Mammoth Cave; and it was with positive regret
that we finally turned away from the fern-fringed chasm
lying there in the soft moonlight, where the sparkling
cascade throws pearly drops from the mossy ridge, and
spreads its mist like a silver veil.

APPENDIX A.

Underground America is of vast extent, and we have much yet to learn as to the varieties of life permitted by its peculiar conditions. Vegetation in Mammoth Cave would be seriously affected by its hydrography. As the primitive river system of the Ohio Valley sank from terrace to terrace, the floor of the cavern would sink from tier to tier. There are in all five well marked levels; the lower ones being still liable to inundation, but the upper ones being extremely dry. In arid localities, destitute alike of light and of moisture, few plant forms could grow. Wood decays slowly; meat hung up remains long without putrefaction; luncheon relics, though there by the cart-load, impart not the slightest taint to the atmosphere. But in the lower halls, where the conditions are reversed, timbers soon decay and meat quickly spoils. From the underside of bridges masses of snow-white fungi many feet long sway in huge fantastic folds. Five indigenous kinds of fungi have been thus far identified; by far the most common being the *Oozonium auricomum.* I found a bed of agarics near the river Styx, which led to experiments for raising mushrooms on a large scale for the markets. The prepared beds are to be seen in Audubon avenue, where thousands of dollars have been expended under expert gardeners.

The fauna of caverns is richer than their flora. Yet the list is not long after rigorously excluding transient varieties. Bats, rats, mice, and lizards are no more truly cave-dwellers than are the raccoons and opossums that come in to prey on them; although some of them may have staid long enough under ground to be affected by their surroundings. After careful research, and canceling synonymns, I am unable to enumerate more than about one hundred species of true subterranean fauna in the caverns of our country. These are thus distributed through the animal kingdom:

Infusoria	9 species.	Arachnida	31 species.
Vermes	4 "	Myriopoda	5 "
Crustacea	11 "	Insecta	33 "
	Vertebrata	4 species.	

Insignificant as many of these creatures may seem, shyly darting into crevices, or hiding under stones, at the visitor's approach, they have probably had more attention from scientific men than any other animals of their size. They have been microscopically examined down to their minutest particles, and many pages have been laboriously written about them, bristling with words big enough to describe whales and mastodons, instead of minnows, crickets, spiders, flies, worms, and fleas. Those desiring to pursue the matter more thoroughly are referred to the publications of Putnam, Wyman, Cope, Hubbard, Emerton, and others, and especially to the exhaustive memoir on the cave fauna of North America laid before the National Academy of Sciences, in 1886, by Professor A. S. Packard, together with a complete bibliography of cave literature.

Only a few of the many hard names given by scientists to the animals of Mammoth Cave need be mentioned to the general reader. Amblyopsis, Typhlichthys, and Chologaster are generic appellations of the blind fish. The sightless crawfish is the Cambarus pellucidus. The formidable name of the cave cricket (or grasshopper) is the Hadenoecus subterraneus. The ordinary cave spider is the completely eyeless Anthrobia; and there are also the Acanthocheir, the absurdly long-legged Phrixis, and perhaps one or two other species. The flies for which these spiders lie in wait are the Anthomyia, and the singularly interesting Phora. Among beetles may be mentioned the Adelops and Anophthalmus; while the Myriopods are represented by the hairy Scoterpes and its near ally the Pseudotremia. Cave hunters will be gratified to learn that none of these creatures are known to be poisonous. I never heard of any serpents venturing within the cave; and the few lizards that one sees are harmless. Its fastnesses harbor no wild beasts, whatever may have once been true as to bears and panthers, wolves and wild cats.

What do cave animals feed upon? The Myriopoda subsist on decaying wood, and the debris swept in by streams. Crickets also live on decaying vegetable matter. But the majority of cave animals are scavengers, feeding on the relics left by human visitors. Spiders spin their webs in the dark to catch silly flies. Blind crawfish live on the Crangonyx and other minute crustacea, on which also the eyeless fish likewise feed, as well as on the young crawfish, when these can be caught, and on minnows of their own species. They have been kept for a year in an aquarium with no food except the convervae and animalculae growing naturally in the water.

All kinds of cave fauna tend to deterioration. The plants are bleached. The spiders, flies, and centipedes are either a pale brown or white. The fish are translucent. We do not recall an exception to this general rule. Seemingly the cells are absorbed in which the light should have secreted pigmental matter. Sightless animals, however, show differences indicating a progressive adaptation to their environment. They also enjoy some peculiar compensations for the atrophy of their organs of vision, in the increased sensitiveness of their other organs, and in the remarkable elongation of their hair, antennae, and limbs. Their habits are extremely wary. Put the common crawfish in the same tank with the blind variety; offer the same food to both; by the former it will be taken eagerly and disposed of, but the latter will dart back, wave its long feelers for further information, and only take the morsel after a series of cautious approaches and retreats.

As to the age of the cavern Fauna, some authorities carry it back to the Cretacious period, others to the Tertiary, and others again no further than the early Quaternary. I incline toward the more modern date. Comparisons have been worked out between the cavern Fauna and certain abyssal species from the Alpine lakes, the Caspian Sea, and deep oceanic soundings. But after all the cavern region must have been insular, at a time when its surroundings were marine or lacustrine. That being so, its life would be characteristic of that period whose retreating waves made the insular region possible, which was presumably the Quaternary. Insulation would result in isolation; and that amid disadvantages fatal to weak or inflexible species, and modifying stronger ones. Surviving forms would gradually become adapted to their peculiar environment by a process more fitly described as retardation than as development.

Why, under what we regard as a benign administration, should certain species be imprisoned as denizens of darkness for successive generations, spanning thousands of years, until the beautiful organs once enabling their ancestors to enjoy the blessed light, should have wasted away and totally disappeared? A partial answer is found in the wonderful compensations that manifest the constant working of a benevolent design, even amid extraordinary obstacles. Some problems that used to be deemed insoluble have been clearly solved; and others that now are dark will yet be made clear for men who have patience to wait and work and think. Meanwhile let us rejoice in the infinite variety of revelations actually made to our growing minds, whether from the starry skies, the abysmal seas, or from the labyrinthine caves and subterranean streams.

APPENDIX B.

THE OPENING OF GANTER AVENUE.

If the reader will find on the general Map of the Cave, the localities designated as the Wooden Bowl Room (25), and the Serpent
Hall (45), he will better understand the significance and importance
of Ganter Avenue, the name now given to a combination of several
smaller avenues, effected by sixteen months of hard labor under Mr.
H. C. Ganter's direction, and plotted by H. C. Hovey and Ben
Hains, March, 1891. The history of this passage-way is peculiar. In
September, 1879, certain guides returning from the end of the cave,
noticed, on reaching Serpent Hall, that smoke was issuing from a
crevice to which their attention had not previously been called.
They were naturally excited, as they could not imagine the cause of
such a phenomenon, suggesting some sort of internal fire. But having
crossed Echo river to the shore nearest the entrance, they found workmen there pitching a boat, and by that means creating a great smoke
not perceived on the river. This showed that there must be some
secret connection between the two places. Going back to Serpent
Hall they wormed their way through a series of extremely narrow
crevices, finally emerging by the Black Snake Avenue into the Wooden
Bowl Room. To this new discovery I gave the name of Welcome
Avenue; but now, with permission, re-name the entire combination
Ganter Avenue, in honor of the manager, by whose tireless energy
and engineering skill it has been opened for the public. In doing this
feat obstacles were overcome that seemed insurmountable.

For a long distance the passage, though thirty or forty feet high,
was extremely narrow at the bottom, besides being as crooked as possible. A new stone floor was boldly laid midway to the top where a
wider path was secured. Yet even then the walls converged at places
so as to compel one to go sidewise for a hundred yards at a time; and
when two men met, one of them would have to lie down and let the
other walk over his body. The walls, moreover, were frequently
studded with countless knobs from two to five inches long, and sharp
enough to make a careless passer quite uncomfortable. At no small
cost, and by much judicious digging, pounding and blasting, these and
other obstacles have been overcome, so that the entire avenue is now

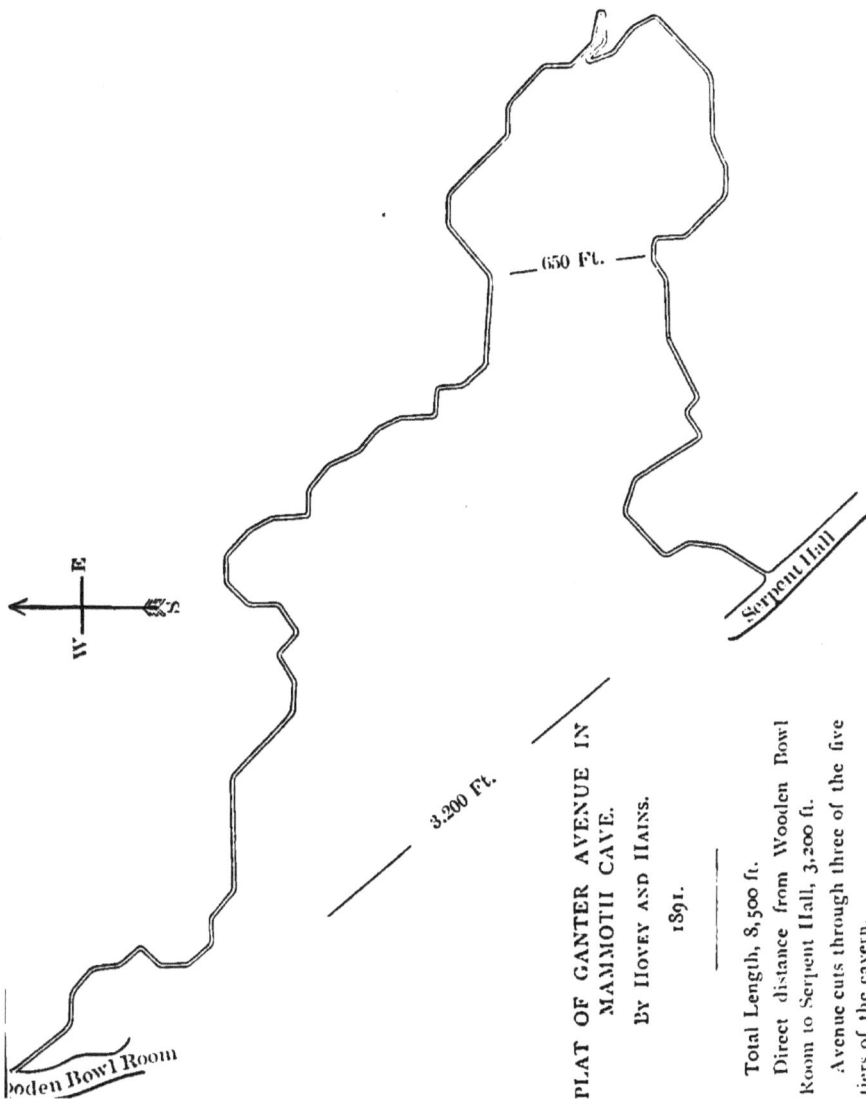

PLAT OF GANTER AVENUE IN
MAMMOTH CAVE.

By Hovey and Hains.

1891.

Total Length, 8,500 ft.
Direct distance from Wooden Bowl
Room to Serpent Hall, 3,200 ft.
Avenue cuts through three of the five
tiers of the cavern.

650 Ft.

3,200 Ft.

Serpent Hall

Wooden Bowl Room

easily passable. Among the remarkable triumphs of engineering, especially remembering the narrow quarters of the workmen, is the construction of what we have called Rider Haggard's Flight (for the author of that remarkable cave-novel "She"); a stairway of one hundred solid stone steps connecting the three levels of the cavern. There are branches from the avenue leading to domes, pits and crystal rooms, etc. But the main advantage of the passage is that it enables the manager to send parties over the Long Route at any time of the year, regardless of the condition of the rivers. Ordinarily tourists would much prefer to go by River Hall, on account of the fine echoes, as well as other objects of interest. But when the streams are flooded, Ganter Avenue will always be found dry and safe. The direct rock distance from the Wooden Bowl Room to Serpent Hall is estimated at about 3,200 feet; but such are the manifold windings of Ganter Avenue, that its entire length, as measured by us, is exactly 8,500 feet, although to a weary visitor, longing for the comforts of the hotel after a day's journey under ground, it would probably seem to be twice that distance

www.ingramcontent.com/pod-product-compliance
Lightning Source LLC
Chambersburg PA
CBHW021416090426
42742CB00009B/1155